For
LOVE
and
MONEY

For
LOVE
and
MONEY

One couple's story of love, ambition, perseverance, and the founding of Southern Financial Bank

By Georgia Derrico
Rod Porter

Quaderer Media Group
175 Varick Street
New York, NY 10014

For Love and Money

Copyright © 2025 by Georgia Derrico and Rod Porter
All rights reserved.

No part of this book may be reproduced, stored in a retrieval system, or transmitted in any form or by any means – electronic, mechanical, photocopying, recording, or otherwise – without prior written permission from the publisher, except by a reviewer who may quote brief passages in a review.

Published by Quaderer Media Group
175 Varick Street, New York NY 10014
www.quaderer.com

First Edition: May, 2025
ISBN: 979-8-9916659-2-6

Cover design by Claudine Mansour

Library of Congress Control Number: 2025939577

The information in this book is based on the author's experience and research. While the author and publisher have made every effort to ensure that the information in this book is accurate, they cannot assume responsibility for errors or omissions, nor are they liable for any loss or damage arising from reliance on the information contained herein.

For information about special discounts for bulk purchases, please contact info@quaderer.com.

Printed in the United States of America

Sandler O'Neill & Partners, L.P.

919 Third Avenue, 6th Fl., New York, NY 10022
Tel: 212.466.7819/800.635.6855
Fax: 212.466.7984
jdunne@sandleroneill.com

James J. Dunne III
Senior Managing Principal

November 5, 2003

Ms. Georgia S. Derrico
Chairman & Chief Executive Officer
Mr. R. Roderick Porter
President & Chief Operating Officer
Southern Financial Bancorp, Inc.
37 East Main St.
Warrenton, VA 20186

Dear Georgia and Rod,

Congratulations on a successful conclusion to a well thought-out plan. It is an extraordinary achievement. To think you started this bank in your garage 18 years ago with $4 million in capital from family and friends -- and proceeded to create a financial enterprise valued today at a third of a billion dollars!

We are thrilled with the market's reaction to the deal, and we have received much positive feedback from our institutional clients.

Thank you for giving us the opportunity to advise your company. We see this move as the beginning of a new chapter and are committed to working with the new Provident / Southern team. We fully expect this to become one of the premier franchises in the Mid-Atlantic region.

All of us at Sandler O'Neill are proud of our long affiliation with Southern and, given our history, this transaction carries much significance. Herman loved spending time with you both and this deal would have made him all smiles. Everyone here at Sandler O'Neill shares in wishing you the best.

Sincerely,

God Bless America,
Jimmy

P.) Herman Sandler has a big smile! He would be so happy and proud of you both on this deal!

Sandler O'Neill & Partners, L.P., is a limited partnership, the sole general partner of which is Sandler O'Neill & Partners Corp., a New York Corporation.

Written by Jimmy Dunne at Sandler O'Neill. When he says "Herman has a big smile," he's referring to Herman Sandler, the founder of Sandler O'Neill, who was a good friend. Herman passed away in the 9/11 attacks on the World Trade Center.

Contents

CHAPTER ONE - Pre-Game   1

CHAPTER TWO - Ground Game   21

CHAPTER THREE - The Passing Game   67

CHAPTER FOUR - The Endgame   125

CHAPTER FIVE - The Post Game   151

CHAPTER SIX - Post Game Analysis   161

APPENDIX   189

CHAPTER ONE
PRE-GAME

Pre-Game

Rod: In the beginning, at least for me, it was all about sex. Love and money came later. (For more on the money part, see Appendix A at the end of the book: "Celebrating 10 years of Success at Southern Financial.")

I'd worked at the old Chemical Bank since 1966. Georgia had worked there since 1971, but our paths had never crossed. Georgia was in the Mets (the lowly Metropolitan Division) and I was in the elite International Division.

Georgia*: The Metropolitan Division was where Chemical generated all of its earnings! The International Division was a total waste. You guys had no idea how to lend money.*

Rod: I actually thought she was a guy. In 1976, I was Chemical Bank's General Manager in Tokyo and I got a telex from "George A Derrico" about Steuber Japan, which was one of her clients. For those of you who grew up with faxes and e-mails, telexes were how we communicated internationally. We gave the handwritten text of your message to an operator who typed it into a machine about the size of a Shetland pony. On the other end it came out in rolls of paper. In 1976, telex operators weren't used to women sending important messages.

A quarter century later, it's hard to remember what a men's club banking was back then, and how fast it changed. At the last International Division Officers' Christmas Dinner, which I attended before I transferred to Tokyo in 1975, there were no women at all in attendance.

For many years, Chemical had conducted an annual six-week program for its most promising managers. In 1977, women participated for the first time. Georgia and Susan Webb were both newly minted Vice Presidents in the Corporate Division. They joined about 20 men in the Chemical Bank Executive Management Program at Harvard. Fortunately, I was among the 20 men.

On the first night there was a cocktail reception for all the attendees. Despite a serious case of jet lag attributable to a flight from Tokyo, I was immediately disabused of the fact that she was a guy.

At that cocktail reception, Georgia awoke in me simple, primitive sexual desire — and a quarter century later she still does, in spades. I'd been in an unhappy marriage for 13 years, but had been as faithful as a choirboy. However, that evening, I knew I had to have her in the biblical sense. Had I been a Neanderthal I'd have just hit her over the head and dragged her to my cave. Yuppies in 1977, though, were supposed to be more sensitive.

It was not easy. After a large group dinner a couple of days later, Jim Good — one of the Chemical Bankers at the program and a legendary bad actor in the real estate division — and I managed to shed all the other males at the seminar but retain Georgia and Susan Webb. However, Jim was spontaneously paired with Georgia, and I was paired with Susan. I had to fix that quickly.

In the most momentous bathroom break of my life, I was standing next to Jim at the urinals at a Boston nightclub. Trying to make it a joke, I told Jim that I was the senior officer and that when we left the urinals, I would be together with Georgia and he would be with Susan. He agreed. (Jim remains a good friend to this day and was a customer of Southern Financial Bank for all of its 18 years. I think Georgia is still mad that he gave up so easily.)

Georgia and I had a tempestuous courtship. We had our first fight about a week later in Marblehead, Massachusetts. That is why we named our farm Marblehead Farm.

After the first three weeks of the Harvard program, I went back to Tokyo and was then reassigned to London. I managed to keep our long-distance romance going from there.

Georgia: I'd applied to Chemical Bank shortly after Rod joined and got a letter telling me that they didn't hire women in the International Division, despite the fact that I had a Masters degree in International Affairs from SAIS at Johns Hopkins. Rod didn't have a Masters degree in anything, but he got a job in the International Division. I finally got an interview in the Bank for the

Pre-Game

Metropolitan Division through a friend of my father. After a full day of interviews I was offered a position in the officers training program at a salary of $9,000 a year — $1,000 less than I was earning as a teacher. I took the job and never gave it a second thought.

I'd had an absolutely wonderful career working myself up through the ranks and getting promoted in various reorganizations. By the time I went to Harvard, where I met Rod, I was shortly to be made Head of the National Division District responsible for New England. Susan and I were the first women to be made National Division District Heads. That was huge. I was on top of the world and my career was taking off. It felt good and uncomplicated, and I was eager to grab it and move on.

But my personal life was in absolute shambles. My first husband, Peter Derrico, had failed medical school in Italy and was struggling in his career. He resented that I was having so much fun and doing so well in my career at Chemical.

Rod: After 18 months in London, I was reassigned to New York and got promoted to Senior Vice President Asset/Liability Management. Given the time, and the fact that no one really knew anything about interest rate risk at the time, it was the ultimate stress job. But I continued to pursue Georgia and was ultimately successful.

Georgia: *When Rod got back from London he went into a full-court press and I willingly succumbed. It was incredibly difficult. I was the eldest daughter in a close Italian-American family. I had two younger sisters and three younger brothers. My mother was so paranoid about divorce that when any woman at the Westchester Country Club divorced she never talked to them again. No woman in our family on either side had ever had a divorce.*

My parents adored my first husband. Peter was an Italian-American and we lived just three blocks from my parents. He was a golfer like the rest of my family, and would play often with my father and my brothers. (**Rod**: Golf is the only vice I don't have.) *To top everything off he joined the Westchester Country Club. At the time women couldn't be members on their own.*

Rod didn't have a drop of Italian blood. He didn't golf. He lived in Connecticut, not Westchester County. (My mother was convinced there were still Indians in Connecticut.)

Rod: We finally got married in 1982. We tried to get married in the Episcopal Church in Greenwich, Connecticut. As is always the case the Episcopal Church is the nicest in town and the one in Greenwich was no exception. My mother had called her Bishop in Kentucky who arranged an introduction in Greenwich. Her Bishop had arranged for us to meet a young Episcopal minister who was to counsel us. We were in our 30s and he was in his 20s. We met him one night and he had a velvet cape and desert boots and wanted to counsel us. He was not to be the person who married us.

Rose, Georgia's mother, found another minister and he married us at the Westchester Country Club on February 6, 1982. We were never sure whether he was a minister or a distinguished actor. Only Rose knows for sure. What was important was we got officially married.

The wedding was an absolute blast. We had all of our friends at Chemical and both of our families. My son Trent was our best man, my daughter Vanessa was the maid of honor, and our son Devon was the ring bearer. The symbolism that Devon represented was very powerful. Over the next 20 years he became our bond. Later on, when he was 10 years old, he decided he was going to become our son, and he did. Today, Devon is Georgia's son. Period. He's not her biological son, but neither one of them thinks in those terms.

Pre-Game

During the ceremony, Devon created the suspense. He teetered on the step and almost fell down. He was only 3 years old.

Devon

We had a harpist before the ceremony whom we told to play Bach. After the ceremony we had a hard rock country music band. There were tables with caviar and sushi — a bit ahead of its time but received very well. We were finally out of our closet at Chemical Bank. Everyone who mattered at the Bank was there except Tom Johnson, my boss. He was a religious man — he attended the Union Theological Seminary — and was probably conflicted.

Rod, Me, Jim Good, my brother Charles and David deGive

Pre-Game

Georgia: *Fast forward to 1984 and I thought I'd finally made it. I was Senior Vice President — Corporate Affairs. I was so proud of myself. It was a staff job where I was responsible for managing four different departments. I was reporting to Dick LeBlond, Vice Chairman of the bank, and hated it. I was dying to get back to a line job where I would be dealing with customers. I interviewed with Bob Lipp and Bob Callander. It was during what we called the ecumenical Presidency of the bank when we had three Presidents, a Catholic, a Protestant and a Jew. It wasn't the ecumenical nature of the arrangement which was a problem. The problem was that you can't have three Presidents. The experiment was short-lived.*

Bob Lipp offered me a job, but it was a demotion. Bob Callander offered me a staff job, but I'm not really at my best in those kinds of roles. Tom Johnson, the Catholic, didn't offer me anything. (So much for Catholic solidarity.)

I discussed these with Rod and he said, "You will go crazy with either of these jobs. Life is too short. Why don't you say no and if necessary you can quit." He made sense and suggested that I think about starting a bank like our friend Steve Duckworth was. I wanted to do something entrepreneurial. I loved managing and motivating people. I liked dealing with customers in different industries. I knew I wanted to do something different, but it was natural for me to stay in banking. I'd reached a very senior level at Chemical for a woman and knew that future promotions would be slow going. More than anything I liked the idea of being my own boss.

Rod: She "liked the idea of being my own boss." It sounds simple and upbeat, but in retrospect it was a huge leap of faith. Georgia had been trained at Chemical to be a superb commercial banker. She'd risen as far as any woman had risen in a line job. She had utterly no experience being an entrepreneur — but as it turned out being an entrepreneur came naturally for Georgia.

Georgia: *I called my parents to tell them I was leaving Chemical and going out on my own. They weren't pleased. My mother said, "You're crazy. You have a great job at Chemical. Why leave?" I said I'd made up my mind and had already told Chemical. My mother said, "No, Georgia, go tell them you'll stay." I hung up depressed, but also determined to go ahead.*

In retrospect I understand my parents' perspective. I was 36 years old, a Senior Vice President at the fifth largest bank in the US. I was making over $100,000 a year, which was a lot of money.

My grandfather, Michael Santangelo, had immigrated from Italy and had been a very successful entrepreneur in New York City. He had an Irish-American bar and a poultry store. (He'd even started a bank, though I didn't learn that until recently.)

But he'd been determined to see all of his children be professionals, not entrepreneurs. He'd sent my father and his nine siblings to universities and graduate schools. One uncle was a New York state judge. Another was a US Congressman in Kennedy's class — unfortunately a Democrat. The rest, except for my father, were teachers, lawyers and a famous surgeon. My father was the youngest and he became a dentist. None of them were entrepreneurs. (My father tried real estate development for a year, but didn't make any money and went back to dentistry.) Was I crazy to leave a great job and go out on my own?

When we got to the actual capital raising my parents were actually very supportive. My father invested $50,000 in the initial offering and another $10,000 in the second offering, which was a lot of money for them. He never sold any stock and he was always proud of me, even though he would exaggerate my success. When Southern Financial had 15 branches he would tell his friends, "My daughter has a bank with 20 branches." When I would say we had only 15 branches he'd tell me, "If I had known you had 15 branches, I would have told them 30. I thought you only had 10."

Dad passed away before we sold the bank. My brother Michael was as close to Dad as I was. After the sale was announced, Michael emailed me: "Congratulations on the sale! It might sound corny, but I think that Dad is looking down at you with a big smile. He is so proud of you."

Tears rolled down my cheeks when I read the message. As I write this, I get teary-eyed again.

Rod: She and I were young, naïve and believed we could do anything. It was a lot harder than we'd bargained for, but the rewards were ultimately a lot greater than we could have anticipated. We plunged ahead.

Pre-Game

As Georgia mentioned, an old friend, Steve Duckworth was well along the track to starting an S&L in Florida. I'd known Steve since the time he'd been in charge of Asset/Liability Management at Southeast Bank in Miami. He has a PhD — not an MBA — from Harvard Business School. (That probably disqualifies him from ever doing anything serious and I've told him that to his face.)

To his credit Steve raised the capital to start an S&L in Florida. He had a gimmick, which compels me to recall Porter's first law: "Never base a business plan on a gimmick." Steve's gimmick was that his branches weren't going to have any cash. They would convince the retirees that they would save so much by not having cash that they could afford to pay higher rates on deposits. He got a ton of publicity from the gimmick in the beginning. In the end, it wasn't the gimmick that killed him. It was a lot of other mistakes — though the gimmick didn't exactly keep him alive.

Georgia: *Steve had called Rod to ask if we would invest in his bank. We were considering it, but we really didn't have a lot of money at the time. Rod suggested I go and visit Steve in Florida for a few days. We wanted to understand what he was doing. If we liked it, we would invest with Steve — and do what he was doing or a variant of it by ourselves. Steve agreed and we scheduled for me to visit with him. Rod sent him $25,000 as our investment in Investors Federal Savings Bank. (Steve did send me a $25,000 check for an investment in Southern Financial, but put a stop payment on the check and never did invest in the bank. Steve's bank, Investors Federal Savings, was taken over by FSLIC early on during the S&L crisis and we lost our $25,000, but I did learn a ton about starting a bank.)*

So I flew to Florida and Steve picked me up at the airport. We got in his car and he tried to start it, but he'd run out of gas. I should have realized then that he had absolutely no common sense. I spent three days with him and learned several things. He told me about Kaplan Smith, a firm who helped with the writing of a business plan and helped get the plan filed. He told me that he was going for a savings charter since it was easier. Also, with a savings charter you were able to borrow from the Federal Home Loan Bank — not, at the time, a commercial bank.

This proved to be important since, initially, one needed to leverage the capital with borrowings since deposits took a long time to get. Steve showed me a credit that one of his founding organizers had proposed to him. I looked at it and said it was awful. He agreed, but indicated it would be awkward for him to turn it down since the guy who proposed it was his director. I learned a valuable lesson and kept to it: No directors would ever be able to borrow from Southern Financial. We would arrange for them to borrow from another bank if necessary. That proved invaluable since one of my founding directors got into financial trouble. Thank God Southern Financial was not involved. Having no insider loans was something we were very proud of and this always made the regulators very happy.

Steve had complicated investment strategies, which, thankfully, I never quite understood. But all in all Steve helped me get started on the path that eventually led to Southern Financial's founding.

I left Florida excited and brimming with lots of ideas. I had Steve's business plan and a lot of other how-to stuff clutched in my hot little hand. My first step was to write an outline of my own business plan to give to potential founding directors in order to get some seed money. I needed seven founding directors, including myself. Steve had volunteered to be one, but warned me that he could not put up any seed money.

I'd decided that my bank would be in Virginia. Rod and I had bought a farm in a small town in Northern Virginia about 50 miles west of Washington DC. Our farm was near Middleburg, Virginia, a town made famous by Jackie Kennedy during her husband's administration. It would have been too hard to start a bank in New York. It was a much more competitive market. On the other hand, I didn't know a single soul in Virginia.

*Rod was off on a trip to Japan for Morgan Stanley and invited me to come with him. I wrote the beginning of my business plan — a lot of it copied from Steve's since I was new to the whole process — in the lobby of the Okura Hotel in Tokyo. I recalled I was impatient (**Rod**: As always!) and determined to get it done quickly.*

When I returned home I was ready to approach potential founding directors to give me $20,000 each in seed money. (Rod had already agreed to be a director and wrote a check for that amount.)

The first person I approached was Neil Call, an old friend of some eight years. I had met Neil and his wife Elly when I was a loan officer for Gulf and Western.

Pre-Game

Rod: A lot of business is friendship and trust. Georgia and I have been through the wars with Neil. We know absolutely everything about each others' characters. As we write this, 30 years later, we're meeting at the Greenbrier Hotel in West Virginia this Friday to have a fun weekend together and to look at a new investment opportunity. We may or may not invest, but we'll certainly enjoy the weekend. If we do invest, we'll make a ton of money.

Georgia: *In 1974 Neil had just recently become CFO of Gulf and Western and we became good friends. Neil and Elly were the first couple that I introduced Rod to even though they had known my first husband. I was very nervous about asking a friend for money. I sent Neil the proposal about the bank and then drove out to Shelter Island to talk it over with him. He was retired by then — although subsequently he went back to work twice and founded his own company. Neil had read the plan and asked many questions. I was delighted when he said he thought it was a good idea and asked what the next step was. I sheepishly said I needed a check for $20,000. He took out his checkbook and I was on my way. Neil remained a director throughout the whole life of the bank and was clearly a tremendous influence in the bank's success. He was often one of the directors of whom both Rod and I would run ideas off. He was knowledgeable and thoughtful in his quiet way.*

The next person I approached was John Marcellus, the CEO and Chairman of Oneida, a flatware manufacturer in upstate New York. I met John in 1981 when I was district head at Chemical of the northeast region. There was a golf outing that Oneida sponsored yearly, and the Chemical loan officer who reported to me and covered Oneida asked me if I wanted to go. I said yes even though I was not a particularly good golfer. Several days later the loan officer came into my office and said, "Georgia there is a problem. I received a call from the CFO at Onedia and it seems that they have never had a woman play golf at Oneida and they need to uninvite you." He said that John Marcellus was so embarrassed and upset that he was going to call me personally. I responded that that was fine. John did call me and apologized profusely and added that next year there would be women golfers playing. He also stated that he wanted to come to New York and take me out to dinner.

I was not sure what it was all about, but thought I should say yes since Oneida was a good customer of Chemical — and after all John was the CEO. During dinner John asked me if I would consider joining Oneida's Board of Directors. I was flabbergasted and honored. I indicated I would very much like to join, but also told him that I needed to check with Chemical's lawyers and that I would get back to him. Later that week I called John and told him that everything was OK. He set up meetings for me to meet with two other directors, Bill Rockefeller and Tom Choate. I met Bill and Tom for lunch, and before I knew it the Oneida plane was picking me up at Westchester Airport and I was heading to a Board Meeting. There, I was voted unanimously in by the Board. The shareholders subsequently approved my election to the board in May 1982. I remained on the Board even after John retired from it in 1984. I finally left the Oneida board in 2003 when they sold to another company.

I asked John to be a founding director of Southern Financial. He immediately said yes and wrote a check for $20,000. He has taught me so much during the short time we were on the Oneida Board together, and for the much longer time he was on the Southern Financial Board. (He retired from the Board in 2001.) He has been supportive and challenging in his not-so-subtle way. He always has an opinion and lets everyone know it. At the beginning I followed in his footsteps and retained the titles of CEO, Chairman of the Board and President. Eventually, I gave up the title of President twice during Southern Financial's life. First to David Campbell, who joined the bank in 1996 for a short stint, and then to Rod, when he joined us in 1998.

John kept his stock in Southern Financial even after he retired from the Board, even though his investment advisors questioned him about it. He told me he said to his advisors, "Those guys know how to run a bank and I am sticking with them." Thanks John.

The next person I approached to be a founding director was David deGive. David and I had joined Chemical on the same day in January 1971. He worked with me later in the northeast district when Chemical was going through one of their many reorganizations. I called Rod who was in the Treasury division and told him that I had someone I wanted him to hire for Treasury.

David had hung up on the Assistant Treasurer of DuPont. He was brilliant but curt, which is a nice way to say he was a little short on social skills. David had never worked in Treasury, but somehow I knew he would excel there. Rod hired him and he was still with Chemical when Rod and I called him in May or June of 1984 *and asked him over to lunch at the New York Yacht Club. There, we asked him whether he would be interested in becoming a founding director and he said yes. David has remained a director ever since. He also joined Southern Financial as an employee in 1992 and has played a tremendous role in the success of the bank.*

I look back at these three guys and am proud they had so much confidence in me, but what a leap of faith they made.

The last two founding directors were local businessmen who later moved away and left the Board. With their checks secured, I was ready to go.

I had $100,000 in cash. Steve had warned me to keep good records of every expense. For the next two years I learned to watch every penny.

One of the first things I had to get was an accounting firm. I set out and talked to Price Waterhouse and Coopers Lybrand (They were separate firms then). Price Waterhouse was Chemical's auditor and Coopers was Oneida's. I told them I would hire the firm who would help me. I was new to Virginia and I needed names of possible investors and or directors. I knew no one. Tom Walsh, who was a young partner heading the Tyson DC office, sent me an extensive list of their customers and stated he had gotten their permission for me to call them to discuss the bank plan. I was impressed with the quickness and detail of the list. Little did I know how impressive the list was. Herb Morgan, Jerry Halpin and Kathy McLean were among the names. I told Tom I would recommend to our Board in organization that Price Waterhouse be hired. They were and remained our accounting firm with Tom as our partner for many years — until Tom had to call me and tell me that Price Waterhouse was getting out of auditing small banks, which was a sad day for both of us because we had established a strong relationship.

Finding a Location

I needed to locate a site for our first branch. I was working in a one-room office in the garage on the farm. It had cinder block walls, two telephones, a copier and one computer. We had four employees working there for six months until the branch was ready for occupancy.

Unfamiliar with Virginia, I got in my car and drove around for several days. I wanted a visible location with not too many banks but some businesses and good residential developments. I thought it would be beneficial to be near an airport since development would increase there. I looked around National, which was pretty developed and then Dulles. I thought Dulles would be a good choice. Remember, the year was 1984 and Dulles was relatively new. I came across a town named Herndon. I had never heard of it. I called Rod, who was in New York. "I found this new shopping center near a Kmart in a town named Herndon, near Dulles, and they are looking for tenants." Rod in his upbeat manner said, "Go for it!"

The next day I got in my car and pranced into the rental office of A. J. Dwoskin — then, as now, a prominent local developer — and said I was interested in talking to someone about the property on Elden St. in the Kmart center. Bob Solomon came in and I told him that I was starting a bank and was interested in renting the property. They were just beginning construction on the shopping center; Bob told me the price per foot and said that it would probably not be ready until September 1984 when we could do the build out. The timing was excellent for us. I asked him what was the deal with the build out. He said that we could do anything we wanted as long as we paid for it all. I said I was willing to accept those conditions. He looked taken back. "I need references from you," he said. "Why? I told you I am willing to sign the lease," I responded. He told me he had no idea who I was and whether I was legitimate. I look back at that conversation and think how naïve I was. I walked into a commercial rental office, tried to commit to a lease and was surprised I was asked to present references.

Pre-Game

Elden Street Under Construction

Raising Capital

This was a long and difficult process. It started once the private placement memorandum was printed. I developed a list of all the people I knew from work and through family and personal friends. Everyone who I thought could have the wherewithal to cough up the minimal investment of $25,000 was sent a private placement memorandum. (This bought them 2,500 shares of stock.) I had my father who talked to several of his friends. Sometimes I called a person, briefly told them about the offering and said I would like to send them a prospectus. We arranged to have several presentations at different locations to stir up interest with a cocktail party to follow. We had one at the Westchester Country Club; one at the New York Yacht Club; one at the Commonwealth Club in Richmond; two at the Hidden Creek Golf Club in Reston, Virginia; and one at the Red Fox Inn in Middleburg, Virginia. All were well attended and developed interest in the bank. But I was surprised and dismayed at how difficult it was to get someone to actually write a check.

> Georgia Santangelo Derrico
> invites you to a presentation
> on
> Southern Financial Federal Savings Bank
> (in organization)
>
> April 10, 1985
> 6:30 pm
> Westchester Country Club
> Rye, N.Y.
>
> R.S.V.P. (914) 967-4090   Cocktails to follow

Westchester County Club Invitation

One of the contacts Tom Walsh of Price Waterhouse had recommended was Herb Morgan of Lawyers Title. I called Herb and set up a meeting with him. I arrived to the meeting confident and went full force ahead. I told him about my idea for starting a bank. I told him that for only $50,000 he could become a director. I will never forget his expression. He said, "I like what I hear, but I have no idea who you are." I told him I would be happy to give him references. (I'd learned my lesson from the A. J. Dwoskin/Bob Solomon experience.) He said he really was not interested in being a board member, but would be willing to be an investor. He said he would like to propose someone who might be willing to be on our Board: Walter Frankland, who was President of the Silver Users Guild. Rod and I agreed to meet with Walter and his wife at the Rosslyn Marriott. He agreed to join our Board and indicated that he had a friend with whom he had graduated from West Point who might also want to invest. His name was John Byrne, a senior partner with Baker Mackenzie. Rod and I said we were having a presentation at the Hidden Creek Golf Club and we would love for Walter as well as John to come. They came and John joined the Board, too, putting in a substantial amount of money. He also brought in John MacDonald, a colleague from Baker MacKenzie, as another investor.

Pre-Game

The original investors, including us, bought the stock in 1986 for $10 a share. Adjusted for stock splits and stock dividend their basis was about $3.75 a share. When we announced the sale to Provident 18 years later, the price was $44.50 a share. Moreover, Southern Financial paid cash dividends every quarter beginning in 1992. In other words, excluding the cash dividends, the initial investors, including us, received more than a 1,000% return on their initial investment. Quite a story. I'm very proud of that.

The original investors included several stellar names who stuck with us until the end: John Mack, then with Morgan Stanley and a friend of Rod's, now the head of Credit Suisse First Boston; Max Chapman, then head of Kidder Peabody; and David Booth and Brian Walsh, both then Managing Directors of Morgan Stanley.

We networked our friends as well as we could, and were finally able to raise $4 million. It should be noted that the minimum requirement then for capital for a savings and loan was $3 million. This was before the thrift crisis. Although we had the necessary amount we still needed regulatory approval. That took much longer than we'd anticipated. The head of OTS was Ed Gray, who decided he did not want a bunch of new thrifts, so he delayed and delayed. But we finally received regulatory approval on April 11, 1986.

We had to watch the money we spent. We had borrowed over $500,000 from Sovran Bank, as it was then known, based on the personal guaranty of all the founding directors.

During the time I raised capital there was so much more that needed to get done. I came up with a name: Southern Financial Bank. It was probably a bit deceptive since the only thing Southern about me was that Rod and I had owned our farm in Virginia for a year or so. But I wanted to emphasize that we were Southern and appeal to locals.

Once I'd chosen the name we needed a logo. Jim Hillestad, who had headed the Creative Services Department at Chemical and reported to me there, designed the logo we used proudly for the entire life of the bank. Jim also helped us with out our first brochures. He is still a very close friend today and was a stockholder until the end (although he sold some of his stock a little early).

Our deal with our vendors was they did not get paid until we opened. For furniture, I called David Harden from Harden Furniture, who was on the Oneida Board with me. I ordered my desk, a conference table and several other items. He gave me a huge discount and I did not have to pay for several months.

I also needed to resolve the issue of what service bureau to use. Early on, I had learned that thrifts were way ahead of commercial banks in doing their core processing. Commercial banks typically did not outsource, and most had a proof department and therefore were not able to be on real time. By outsourcing thrifts we were on real time, which proved to be an immense advantage with overdrafts, online banking and the like. I got three names of service bureaus and visited Investor Savings Bank in Richmond, which was using Savings & Loan Data Corp. (SLDC). (Ironically, Investors Savings Bank was to fail and be taken over by the RTC. Much, much later we hired Tom Baker, who was Investors' CFO, to run our operation in Charlottesville and Richmond.) I was impressed with the way the core processor worked. I then visited SLDC in Cincinnati and spent two days reviewing their operations. SLDC had started off as a part of the Federal Home Loan Bank system, but had been spun off into a co-op owned by its S&L customers.

We decided to go with them and remained on their system for the next 18 years — although we periodically threatened to move to another core processor if they wouldn't support what we were trying to do. They ultimately changed their name to Intrieve and privatized themselves. By the time we left them we were their largest user and had some clout with their CEO, Jack Kuntz, whom Rod liked a lot. For a long time Intrieve was a strength. It allowed us to offer real-time processing when a lot of much bigger banks could not.

Insurance

Before we could open we needed Directors & Officers (D&O) Insurance. We went to the well-known agency Marsh McLennan and applied for it. We were told that D&O insurance had almost dried up since so many banks and S&Ls were having problems. Marsh McLennan thought they would be able obtain the insurance, but several weeks passed and they were not getting anywhere. They suggested that they go to Lloyds of London. I told them to go ahead; I was getting desperate and although I had not yet received regulatory approval, I knew that I really needed to get D&O for my directors. Marsh McLennan applied to Lloyds again. There were delays. I was beside myself. I asked an agent at Marsh if they thought it would be useful for me to personally fly to London and plead our case. They contacted their connection at Lloyds, who thought that it might be a good idea. So I flew immediately to London and visited Lloyds and got a tour of their operation and pleaded our case. I emphasized the quality of our Board's credentials as well as my background. I received good vibes. I returned back to Virginia and within one week of my departure from London we received a D&O binder. I guess the lesson from this was that it does help to meet people face to face.

CHAPTER TWO
GROUND GAME

Ground Game

Rod: This could have been the ultimate feminist book. Georgia was one of the first women to climb the ladder to the near top in a major American corporation. She was also one of the very few women who climbed the ladder and gave it all up to start her own business. This book is really about how she achieved that and how, together, we were ultimately spectacularly successful in both financial and non-financial terms.

The only problem is that Georgia never had any interest whatsoever in the feminist movement. She never had any doubt that she could do anything she wanted to do. She was the eldest of six kids and was the absolute apple of her father's eye. We have home movies of her at 10 organizing her younger siblings for the "Little/Big Show" at the Westchester Country Club. She hasn't changed in 50 years.

Southern Financial never was a "women's bank" and there were a lot of those that opened in the period when Georgia founded Southern Financial. In fact, Georgia interviewed for the presidency of the "women's bank" in Greenwich, Connecticut, and they gave the job to a guy. I can't think of any of the "women's banks" that survived until the 21st century. It was a stupid idea that was condescending to women, just as the idea of "Black banks" was condescending to Black people. Almost none of the "Black banks" that opened during that era are still around either.

While Southern Financial wasn't a "women's bank" it was always a "wo*man*'s bank." It was Georgia's from the beginning. She never believed she was disadvantaged by being a woman. She simply saw an opportunity and seized it. The feminists who make feminism their career would say that Georgia was a traitor to their cause. (The Black people who make a profession of being Black feel the same way about Colin Powell and Condoleeza Rice.) Georgia single-handedly won the ground game for Southern Financial. In retrospect it was clear why she was going to win.

She went to St. Mary's, the sister school of Notre Dame. Notre Dame's coaches were Knute Rockne and Ara Parseghian. Ronald Reagan was the gipper. They knew how to win games. She was a CEO in their traditions. At Williams College, where I went, our chant was "Repulse them, repulse them, make them relinquish the ball." It was a subtle socialist message. The other team never did relinquish the ball and we really didn't care. And we lost. At St. Mary's and Notre Dame there was a different ethos. Notre Dame's chant was "Hit 'em again! Harder! Harder!" And Georgia bought into that completely. It's not a subtle or nuanced message.

Georgia has an absolutely iron will. That's an easy thing to say, but a harder thing to communicate. When Georgia wants to do something she does it. Southern Financial was her creation from the very beginning. And it was hers until the very end.

Before she proceeds with her narrative, I want to talk about the qualities that are unique to Georgia and ultimately led to Southern Financial's extraordinary success.

- For lack of a better word, Georgia is impatient. As many of you know, her patience is measured in nano-seconds. Her impatience kicks in as soon as the thought hits her brain. She's impatient to get on to the next thing and she's even more eager to leave the last one. She can be incredibly obnoxious when she thinks it's time to go. We're always early for appointments and woe betide you if you're on the phone with me when she decides it's time to leave. She always packs two nights before we leave and when we return from a trip we have to unpack as soon as we get back, before we relax. Her watch is an expensive precision chronometer from Cartier with lots of diamonds, but it's always 10 minutes fast. Impatience, or whatever you want to call it, is simply Georgia.

   I can't talk about this enough. For Georgia it's "let's get it done *now*!" Her people understand that. If they can't, they hate her for it. And "hate" is not too strong a word. You have to understand that Georgia and I weren't easy. We were incredibly tough. Starting a public company is not — repeat, *not* — cakewalk. We made a lot of people rich, which is marvelous. Some of the people who came on board later made a lot of money, too, though in some cases not as much as they wanted.

In Georgia's world, if you can't get it done now it's probably not worth getting done at all. Her impatience meant that Southern Financial made decisions at warp speed. Not all of the decisions were right. But a higher percentage of her decisions were right than if they'd been made by committee. As a consequence, Southern Financial moved twice or three times as fast as any normal financial institution would have moved. That had significant economic value.

- With Georgia you're either on her team or you're on another team. She is fiercely loyal to you if you're on our team. If you're on her team, or are family or a friend, she will protect you with a leonine ferocity you just can't imagine. If you're not on our team, or you're not part of her family or mine, she is an implacable foe. If you want to hurt me, or Devon or Linda, or any of a dozen more people, you have an enemy you can't imagine. There are no neutrals in Georgia's world. If someone is loyal to you, you are loyal to them.

- You know where you stand with Georgia. She's not poker faced — just the opposite. Her "hairy eyeball" is legendary. If she teases you, she loves you. The harder she is on you the better. Beware if she's polite. If she stops talking to you, quit quick.

She teased Bill Lagos more than anyone else. Billy came on board as Controller when Southern Financial was only a year old. For a long time he was the only male at Southern Financial. Georgia adored Billy, but Georgia and the other women teased him mercilessly for 17 years. Billy provided rich material for teasing. He is the world's leading Mr. Malaprop. We wrote down his malaprops over the years because they were too good to lose. Here are some of them:

- "I'm working and you're sitting there in your Eiffel Tower!"
- "Isn't this the tail wagging the body?" or "The tail shaking the dogma?"
- "You're on thick ice here!"
- "My Elmer Mater is Benjamin Franklin College."
- "You're choking my chain!"

- "Stop hoovering over me!"
- "Who do you think you are, Albert Edison?"
- "Let me embalm on that point."
- "You're just riding on my shirtsleeves."
- "I know you've been waiting for this with rebated breath!"
- "If the foot was on the other shoe, you'd feel differently."
- "Frannie Mae"
- "You're ill bent on proving me wrong!"

Billy's aphorisms came to be known as "Billaverbs." Every year at the bank's summer picnic, the women, including Georgia, would get together and throw him in the pool at our farm. He handled the teasing and was Georgia's rock during the early years. I can't tell you how happy she is he ended up a "Rich Greek."

- I said Georgia has an iron will. Absolutely nothing will deter her from doing what she wants to do. In 1996 she learned from her annual physical that she had breast cancer. It was a Friday. I was at FX Concepts in my office in New York, just ready to start on my way back to Virginia for the weekend. I remember getting in the taxi on 57th street and asking the cabby to go to LaGuardia Airport. He looked back at me and, sensing a problem, asked what was wrong. I told him about Georgia's breast cancer, but I was never to tell anyone else. I was devastated.

It felt like an eternity before I finally got to the farm. Georgia was incredibly emotional — her favorite aunt/godmother died from breast cancer. Nothing could have been worse. After I got back to Virginia we spent the weekend trying to marshal our resources. Her exam had been with a doctor affiliated with the Loudoun Hospital where Georgia was Chairman of the Board of Trustees. She knew enough about Loudoun Hospital that she didn't want to go there. Georgia's family rallied around her like a wall. With their help we found a doctor in New York, who turned out to be terrific. Dr. Moore was with Columbia Presbyterian hospital.

Georgia*: Rod and both my parents came to the hospital for my first meeting with Dr. Moore. They sat outside while Rod and I went into his office. He looked at the file that Loudoun hospital sent. It indicated that the tumor had to be removed. Dr. Moore said that I could either have a lumpectomy with radiation and possible chemotherapy or I could have a radical mastectomy. I told him I just didn't have time to be sick. My bank had just gone public and I was entirely responsible for running it. I had no time for radiation and chemotherapy was out of the question. I was leaning toward a mastectomy, although I'm not sure I could have handled it. I asked Dr. Moore what he thought and he said, "Georgia, you're still young. Do a lumpectomy and next year you won't remember you went through this." I went with his recommendation and never regretted it for a minute. But the worst was still ahead for me.*

When I awoke from the surgery Dr. Moore was there and the first thing I said was "No chemo!" Dr. Moore kept on trying to calm me down, but I kept saying no way. Thank God I ultimately didn't need chemo.

Rod: Dr. Moore was superb in every way — and he was a Republican. It was a day after the surgery and everyone had gone home. Georgia couldn't stand the hospital food. So I went down to Il Monello, which is only a few blocks from the hospital and got an incredible takeout dinner with wine and smuggled it into the hospital for the two of us. I loved her then incredibly and I love her now.

Dr. Moore decided she needed radiation following the surgery. He set it up at Georgetown University Hospital with a terrific doctor. The radiation was a low point for Georgia. She felt like a piece of meat. It was incredibly difficult emotionally. She had to go to the Georgetown Hospital five times a week for three months.

Georgia*: Something positive comes from everything difficult. I stayed several nights a week at the Georgetown Dutch Inn — now the Monticello Hotel — on Thomas Jefferson Street. I simply fell in love with Georgetown, despite the circumstances, and Rod did as well. After my ordeal was over,* *we bought a small townhouse there that we loved. For several years before we sold the bank, we spent as much time there as we spent on the farm.*

Rod: Absolutely no one at Southern Financial knew what was happening outside of board member Neil Call. If anyone else on the board or in the bank had known, everything could have broken down. She didn't change her routine, except that she spent five nights a week on the days before her radiation treatments at the Georgetown Dutch Inn. I tried to be there as much as I could, but I was still working in New York.

For the first couple of weeks she had to carry around an intravenous solution in a bulb under her jacket. She went to Oneida with it, to the Oneida Board Meeting on US Air. No one knew.

The only people who ever knew besides Neil were me, her mother and father, and her sister June, and Devon. As I said earlier, she's not big into the victim thing.

Maybe it wasn't politically correct. Maybe she should have gone to breast cancer rallies. Maybe she should have gone on television to proclaim her victimhood, but she didn't. She did her job and she did it extraordinarily well. It was Georgia.

The S&L Crisis

She would need her iron will the next 12 years because in 1984 we made the decision to start the bank with an S&L charter rather than a commercial bank charter. It was probably the right decision at the time, but in retrospect it caused us a lot of heartburn.

A little bit of history: The quasi-government entities Fannie Mae, Freddie Mac and Ginnie Mae ultimately eliminated the thrift industry's raison d'etre. This isn't a politically correct thing to say since everyone is supposed to love Fannie, Freddie and Ginnie. We even gave them cool cuddly names. There were three of them so public ire couldn't be focused on one.

Ground Game

The S&L industry was slow to die because Regulation Q of the Federal Reserve Board limited the rate at which S&Ls could pay on their deposits. On the other side of the balance sheet the S&Ls were restricted with respect to what they could invest in. In other words, they couldn't get in a lot of trouble.

That started to change as early as 1967 when the State of Texas began to allow Texas S&Ls to make up to 50% of their net worth in property development loans. Everything accelerated in 1978 when Congress passed the Financial Institutions Regulatory and Interest Rate Control Act of 1978 (FIRREA). After FIRREA, S&Ls were permitted to invest up to 5% of total assets in each of construction, land development and education loans. Think of it, the average thrift at the time had a net worth of X of assets. Now, for the first time ever, they could invest an amount nearly equal to their net worth in three areas where they had no experience whatsoever.

On October 6, 1979 Georgia and I were in Litchfield, Connecticut, at a bed and breakfast trying to have a relaxing weekend. It was Georgia's birthday. Litchfield is a charming historical town that dates back to early America. We haven't been back since. We drove in to the downtown to buy the newspapers and have a cup of coffee. We read the papers and immediately perceived that it was a "Holy Shit" moment and knew that country had changed forever.

Paul Volcker had announced that the Fed would no longer target interest rates and would instead focus exclusively on the monetary aggregates. In practical terms that meant interest rates were about to spike upward. They did. I'm not one of Paul Volcker's confidants, but no one knows whether the violent shift in interest rates was intended or expected. But spike they did.

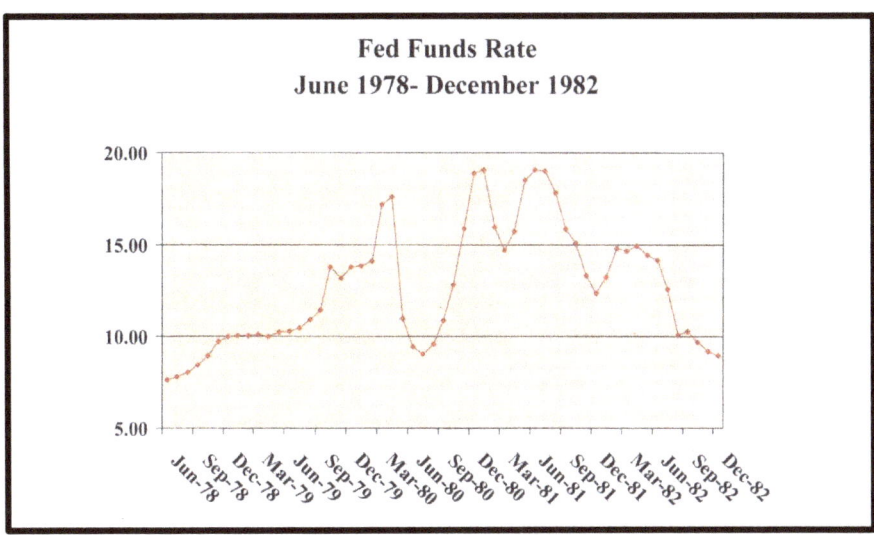

That morning I was worried about Chemical because Asset/Liability Management at Chemical was my job. October 6, 1979 was the most important thing that ever happened to a career Asset/Liability Manager. But it was ultimately much more important to Georgia and me that the October 6 "Volcker Shock" put a lot of S&Ls into an extended swan dive toward oblivion. It probably helped us in the very long run, but it made the bank's early years very difficult.

Volcker's decision was probably the most important public policy decision ever made by an unelected US official. And in retrospect I believe it was probably wrong to do it the way it was done. According to Bert Ely the S&L industry reported losses of $9 billion in 1981 and 1982 combined. Moreover, according to Ely, in mid-1982 the entire industry had a negative net worth of $100 billion, valuing their mortgages at market. Again, I was oblivious to the industry's problems then. I was having enough problems with Chemical's survival. My hair turned gray during this period. But Chemical survived and ultimately prospered.

It got worse for the S&Ls in March 1980. The Carter administration passed the Depository Institutions Deregulation and Monetary Control Act. While it was bad for the S&Ls this was probably the most important and ultimately beneficial economic legislation since the Glass Steagall Act. This law eliminated most of the regulatory distinctions between depository institutions and removed the interest rate ceilings on various types of deposit accounts. It effectively broadened what the S&Ls could do depending on the state where they were operating.

A quarter century later that doesn't seem like a big deal. But at the time it was an earthquake of at least 7.0 on the Richter scale for the S&L Industry. Their worlds were turned upside down. For the first time they could compete for deposits, and for the first time they *had to* compete for deposits. The problem was what they would do with those deposits. You can take all of the deposits you want, but if you have no idea what you're going to do with the money, you have a problem. You can make loans or you can make investments. Both alternatives entail risk. If you don't have the infrastructure to manage the risk, you're dead. Most of the S&Ls didn't have a clue.

Making loans feels easy. If you have people to answer the telephone there are always people and companies who want to borrow money. Real estate developers will always borrow money until the last bank tells them "no." When they get in trouble, they blame their lenders.

In reality, lending money is very difficult. It's an inefficient market, which means there are, in fact, opportunities to make money. But in order to be successful, you have to create an infrastructure and a culture to manage the risk. Since it's not an efficient market, and there are no textbooks and no rules, you can't copy what your competitor is doing because he's probably doing it wrong.

Buying securities, which is the alternative to making loans, also feels easy. As soon as the world knows you have cash every broker in the world will be calling you with investment "ideas." In reality, managing a securities portfolio is as hard as making loans. The spreads are thinner and there is ultimately no margin for error. Moreover, you're playing a zero-sum game with the smartest people in the world, who have an infinite amount of money to spend on computer models, data bases and bright young techies with MBAs. Additionally, there's no question in my mind that it's an efficient market.

In March 1983 Ed Gray was appointed Chairman of the Federal Home Loan Bank Board. He began the process of reversing the deregulatory process for the

S&Ls. In March 1984 the major failures of S&Ls began. Empire Savings Bank of Mesquite Texas failed. It eventually cost taxpayers $300 million.

In March 1985 the Home State Savings Bank of Cincinnati was expected to fail and Ohio's Governor declared a bank holiday, which closed all the state's S&Ls. The S&L industry was crashing.

Georgia: *This was the environment in the Summer of 1985 when the Southern Financial team was finally ready to build the business. We had satisfied virtually all of the requirements for founding except regulatory approval. I thought it was time to hire some employees, but I was running out of money so I had to keep the amount of people on payroll down. The first person I hired was Amy Shannon as branch manager of our first location. She had more than 15 years of banking experience, and was outgoing and knowledgeable. We also hired an assistant branch manager who understood that she would, at times, be a teller. Lastly, we hired a controller. I will never forget the four of us working during the Summer of 1985 in the office — located in my farm's garage, with no air conditioning, no bathroom (we used the one in the house) and only two desks. The other two worked on a couch. We discussed the types of products we were going to offer, hours of operation, marketing materials, supplies and an array of other things. We worked there until November. It was cold and we had to buy space heaters, but our toes never got warm.*

Amy Shannon and Georgia in the garage at the farm

We were ecstatic in November when the Elden Street Branch was ready for occupancy. We packed all of our boxes and said goodbye to our one-room office, which I had personally used for almost two years, for a much more luxurious environment. We had central heating and a bathroom en suite.

We hired a mortgage banker, Dean Kampman, since my background was commercial lending and we were going to have to make residential mortgages. At that time 70% of the bank's assets were going to have to be in residential mortgages. I had no idea how to make a residential mortgage loan. I found Dean through a head hunter named Mike Kirkman, who was quite expensive. I told Mike that I couldn't afford to pay him and he agreed to be paid with bank stock that we issued upon opening.

There we were on our first Christmas in 1985, with a fully furnished office, supplies, $500,000 in debt and $4 million in capital that we could not touch and no regulatory approval. We had our first Christmas Party at the farm. There were six people in attendance. It was fun, but everyone was a little tense.

Christmas came and went and I was getting worried. Money was low. We made it through January, February and March. I did not know how I was going to make payroll for April. Sovereign Bank had extended our line of credit twice, which was guaranteed by our Board. Our law firm was confident that we should be getting regulatory approval shortly.

The call finally came on April 11, 1986, which is ironically Rod's birthday. Someone in the bank said, "Georgia, there is a telephone call for you." I went to answer and a squeaky voice of a little old lady said, "This is the Federal Home Loan Bank; your bank is number 8910." I asked what that meant and she said you can open your bank's doors. I got off the phone and yelled, "We're approved, let's open the doors!" I went up front and opened the doors and lo and behold the first person that walked in was ... a Fed Ex delivery man. He did not want to open an account with us. In fact, no one came in to open an account that day. Despite that, we were all flying high. We'd finally opened after almost two years of preparation.

*Our son Devon visited us that weekend. We told him about the Fed Ex delivery man, and that to that point we'd opened a $500 savings account. (**Devon**: I was only 10, but I remember thinking, "We are in real trouble.")*

Our strategy going forward was simple: We would offer every possible product on the deposit side that we could. We wanted checking accounts, savings accounts, certificates of deposits, and even credit cards — though that's another story. On the asset side, we were going to originate residential mortgages both fixed and adjustable, and sell the fixed rate mortgages in the secondary market. With Rod and David's experience we had developed relationships with some buyers of mortgage backed securities, including Chemical Bank's mortgage subsidiary.

We were going to go and call on all small businesses in and around our shopping center and offer them everything. We thought we could be the best. The "can do" attitude began early on.

We planned a grand opening that was attended by the mayor of Herndon, with balloons, clowns and everything. We decided to give out plastic coffee travel mugs as a promotional gift to new accounts. They were a huge success and we kept them as our promotional gift for several years. Devon still has his.

Georgia and the Mayor

I am proud to say that we were profitable the first full month of operation. This was in part due to my focus on expenses and my penny-pinching style, but also in part due to David and Rod's expertise in asset/liability management.

Rod: This is amazing. Georgia grudgingly gives David and me some credit.

David and I had planned from the beginning to leverage our capital by buying mortgage-backed securities and borrowing from the Federal Home Loan Bank. I know this is incredibly boring, but it is how you make money. David and I did the first interest rate swap ever done by an institution under $5 million in assets. We bought mortgage-backed securities, borrowed from the Federal Home Loan Bank to fund them and then bought an interest rate swap to hedge them. It didn't seem odd when David and I did it but it had never been done before by a bank as small as we were. It gave Southern Financial some earnings on an ongoing basis. It carried Southern Financial for many months until it could get its real game together.

Georgia: *I finally had our first Board Meeting as a bank and not as "in organization." We had a lot of resolutions to approve as well as policies and procedures. I proposed to the Board that I be granted authority to approve loans up to $250,000. Our legal lending limit was $500,000. One of our Directors objected. He thought that was too much authority to give me. I quickly responded — admittedly a little hot under the collar — that at Chemical I had a much larger lending limit. He said he wanted to be part of the process. I said, "You have never made a loan in your life and you are paying me to make those decisions." He said he would like for me to teach him credit. I said that was ridiculous and would not accept that oversight level. The rest of the Board sided with me and I learned early on that to run an effective Board you need to be strong on certain points and not allow them to micromanage.*

Still, over the next several years I looked to the Board to help us in our strategic direction and question us intensively on big decisions. I truly believe that our success was a result of the unique relationship that we had with the Board. The Board was involved in important matters including acquisitions and the openings of new branches. We managed the daily operations of the bank and the Board approved or disapproved directions, policies and new ventures. As a result we were able to move quickly in decision making, and due to the financial sophistication of our Board we were able to take advantage of unique opportunities.

A funny aside, at one of our early Board meetings one of our less-sophisticated Board members was a nit picker and would often raise absurd concerns. He continued to say our signage was too small. I tried to patiently explain that it was out of our control. "The size of the signage is regulated by the Town of Herndon," I explained. At each meeting he raised the issue, again and again. Finally, Rod lost his temper and started yelling that it was a waste of time and there was nothing we could do. The director asked Rod why he was yelling. Rod responded, "Because you are being stupid." The director calmly said, "Thank you Rod, now I understand." This director later was asked to resign from the Board because of his lack of contribution. He did so, but left happy because he made quite a bit on his initial investment.

For the next couple months we concentrated on getting customers, both deposits and loans, and keeping expenses down. We attended Chamber meetings, made cold calls and advertised. It is not easy to get someone to change banks. One thing we learned early on was that the people who showed up when we had just opened a new branch were often deadbeat customers just waiting to pull a fast one on a bank.

The first deadbeat we encountered in Herndon was very interesting in retrospect. At the time I was scared to death. His name was Michael Gilbert and he drove a Mercedes. He came in and asked to see the President. He said he was looking for a small bank and wanted good service and he had lots of deposits going through his various businesses. This was music to my ears. One of his businesses, the only one I recall, was a travel agency. He wanted to know if we took merchant accounts. I stated that we were able to do this. (We had a correspondent relationship then with the Sovereign Bank of Virginia.) He also was looking to refinance his Mercedes. (Another red flag and something we later stopped doing.) We set him up for merchant accounts, opened several checking accounts, gave him a loan application and I thought to myself, "What a great customer." Everything with him went fine for a couple of months. Our first indication of trouble was when Bill Lagos, our SVP controller, came to me and stated that we had received some charge backs — customers telling Visa or MasterCard that they did not get the goods or services they said they'd paid for — on the travel agency accounts. We called Michael Gilbert in and he quickly explained it was a trip that was cancelled and the company he had engaged was difficult to deal with. He assured us that he would take care of it. We believed him and we said that we understood. The overdrafts were taken care of and we relaxed. About a month later, it happened again, and Bill called Michael Gilbert again. This time Bill had a difficult time getting in touch with him, but when he finally did, Michael again reassured him he would take care of it. Now we were suspicious. Bill told me, "I don't like this guy and I do not trust him." I told Bill to visit Michael's office. Bill did and, lo and behold, he'd disappeared. The best we could find out was that he had moved to someplace in Florida where he supposedly had a house. (This is Georgia's first law: Never lend money to anyone with a house in Florida. In Florida, if you go bankrupt you get to keep the house.)

We were never able to locate Michael. We really had no recourse. The charge backs continued and were getting larger. We called Sovereign Bank, which was running the Visa account, and asked how long these returns go on. They said there was no time limit. We told them that the customer had disappeared and we had no recourse. At that time our overdraft for our customer was $65,000. This was a huge amount for us to lose and we could not let it go on indefinitely. We asked Sovereign how this could happen. It seemed Michael Gilbert booked discounted cruises for six months ahead and required a 50% down payment. Customers paid with their Visa cards; their money was credited to Michael's account at Southern Financial. It wasn't until six months later when the customers went to take the cruise that they found out it was cancelled. The customers called Visa and got a refund. Visa, through Sovereign Bank, put a charge through Southern Financial. Since Southern Financial no longer had an account for Michael, it was out the money. Bill Lagos and I talked and both decided this was ridiculous. We could not absorb these losses any longer. There was no telling how long this would go on.

We had numerous meetings with the people at Sovereign Bank, but we were getting the run around. They told us that, under Visa regulations, we were responsible. We responded that we never signed anything. Visa's agreement and our agreement were with Sovereign. In the end, we closed our account with Sovereign and hoped and prayed that was the end of it, but then Sovereign actually filed a lawsuit against Southern Financial. I was devastated. In all my years at Chemical I had learned that banks did not typically sue each other. There was an understanding *among banks that you tried to work out any differences amicably. I called Sovereign Senior Management and then wrote a letter to the President of Sovereign saying that banks do not sue each other. It was counterproductive. I asked if we could not come to some resolution. Much to my dismay I never got a response. So much for banks being reasonable. I proceeded to find a local law firm that had experience in UCC and Visa law. I succeeded in getting a pretty aggressive law firm that managed to charge what I thought was a fortune. They did manage to get a favorable ruling and Sovereign had to pay us back $20,000, but the law firm charged us $10,000 so we netted $10,000 against our $65,000 loss. A lesson learned: Visit your customer's place of business.*

(See Appendix B for an article from *Georgetown and Country* magazine – it was around this time that Georgia was named one of the best dressed women in Washington!)

The National Dance Institute's Visit to Herndon

A much more positive memory from this time was when a group of Chinese children came to Herndon. While I worked at Chemical Bank I joined the Board of the National Dance Institute, which was run by a wonderful, charismatic ballet dancer, Jacques D'Amboise. The National Dance Institute brought the experience of dance to inner city children, which culminated in a gala at Madison Square Garden every year. In 1987 Jacques arranged to have a group of children from China come to the US and participate in the National Dance Institute's annual event. This was a big deal because it was at the beginning of the thaw in US-China relations, first set in motion with President Nixon's visit to China 15 years earlier.

I thought it would be wonderful PR if I got the kids to visit Southern Financial in Herndon. I spoke with Jacques and found out that they were free one night for dinner. He said it should be a very simple, casual dinner since there were some 20 students with the chaperones and others. There would be almost 50 people to feed. My branch manager Amy Shannon and I began to plan. We decided that the branch could not fit 50 people, so we decided to use the parking lot outside the branch. Amy went to get permission from the town of Herndon. Since the Bank was new and did not have too much to spend, we went around and asked the local Chinese restaurants to provide one dish of food. We decided to trailer in one of our old Morgan horses from our farm, High Fashion, so the children could ride. High Fashion was old then, but as I write this 17 years later, she is still alive. She's ancient now.

We bought fabulous balloons, noise makers and candy. The night of the event, dinner tables were set up in the parking lot. Thankfully, it did not rain, but we encountered another problem. The platters from the Chinese restaurants arrived and they turned out to be pretty skimpy. I looked at Amy and said in a panic, "There isn't enough food. We need to get something to supplement it." We pondered what Chinese children might like to eat and we really had no idea. Amy said, "Tuna fish and bread. All kids like it and it is cheap." Hesitantly I gave in and off she went to the Safeway. She came back and quickly made a huge bowl of tuna salad. The children arrived and gave little gifts to all of us.

All of the kids and most of their chaperones lined up to ride High Fashion. They were from Beijing and most had never seen a horse. The tuna fish was a big hit. All in all, it was a great PR feat. The Herndon paper headline was "Chinese Kids Visit Herndon," followed by an article mentioning Southern Financial Bank. And it did not cost us very much even with the tuna salad.

Georgia and the Children

Our First Branch: Middleburg

We had not completed our first full year of operations when Rod started bugging me about opening a branch. I must admit that it was his idea to open a branch in Middleburg. We lived then and still do in The Plains, which is about three miles from Middleburg, an exclusive town known for its wealth. At that time there were only two banks in Middleburg: Middleburg National, which opened in 1924, and Farmers & Merchants, which opened in the late 1800's. The story goes that several years earlier, another bank tried to open there and both banks stopped them by objecting on the basis that there was not enough business to warrant another bank. Middleburg Bank is a terrific bank. We banked there personally before we opened Southern Financial and after we sold it we reopened our accounts and banked there again.

At the time there was a requirement that a bank post a notice in a local newspaper before it could obtain regulatory approval to open a branch. Middleburg had no local paper and was served by The Washington Post and the Washington Times. At the time, virtually no one in Middleburg read the Washington Times, so we placed our ad there over Fourth of July weekend. There were no comments and we received regulatory approval shortly thereafter. When John Palmer, then Senior Vice President of the Middleburg Bank, heard we'd gotten approval, he called me and asked me why we didn't have to advertise. I told him that we had — in the Washington Times. He laughed and said we'd really snuck it through. He was right to be concerned because we ultimately ate their lunch.

When we opened that branch in mid-1987 Southern Financial had just completed our first full year of operations. We had earnings of around $300,000 and total assets of $40 million. The Middleburg Bank, which had a 63-year head start, housed total assets of $100 million and had earned an awesome (to us) $2,000,000. In 2003, the year before we sold, our earnings were $13,184,000. Middleburg's was $8,219,000. We had long since surpassed them in terms of size. The tale of the tape during the intervening 16 years looks like this:

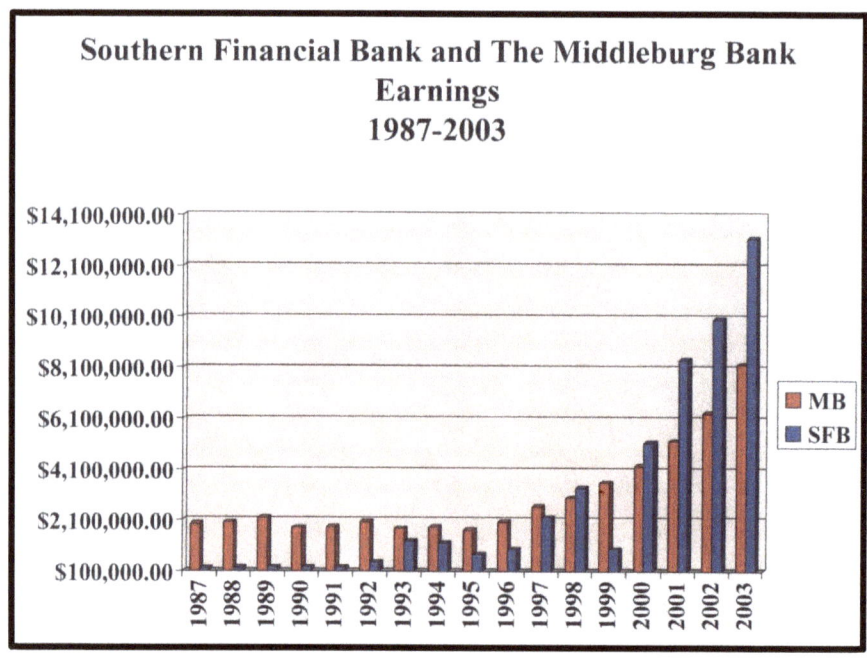

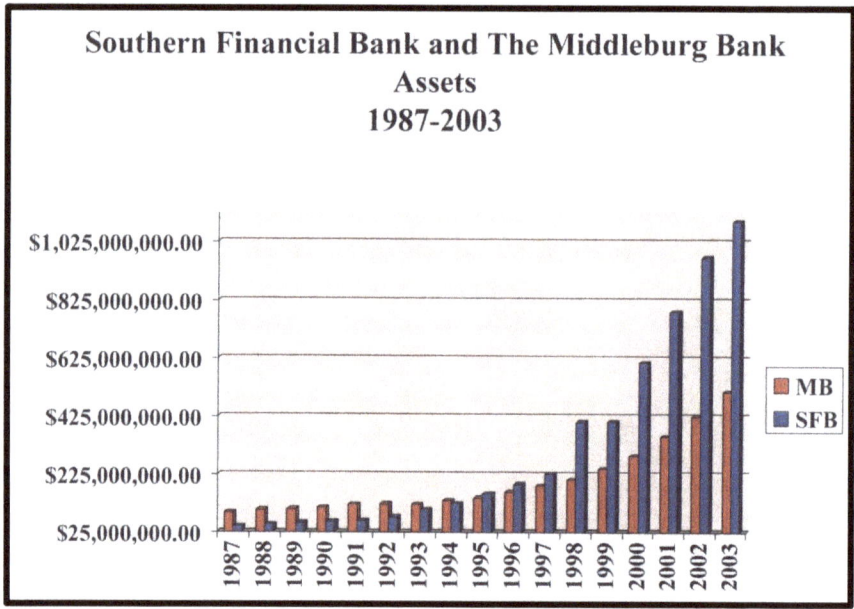

We negotiated a lease for the new branch's space with Nancy Reuter, who owned several buildings in Middleburg, including the famous Red Fox Inn. The Reuter family lived on a farm near Aldie, Virginia, which has been in the family for 200

years. Nancy was a bright, tough negotiator, but I really wanted the space and accepted her terms. Her son Jock was a realtor whose office was in the space, but when Nancy got her deal, she prevailed upon Jock to move next door. It turned out that Jock's sister Diana was an architect who had designed his office. I hired Diana to design the branch and that began a very long and close relationship. She designed several of Southern Financial's branches as well as our main office. She taught me a lot about designing and decorating, cost-efficiently, and was responsible for the development of Southern Financial's signature look with interior windows, green marble, wood floors, and traditional molding and wainscoting. (Diana also designed a very large addition to our home in The Plains.) As it turned out Diana's design was spectacular, despite the preppy local builder we hired to execute it. He overshot his budget from the beginning. The last straw came two weeks before a meeting to go over the remaining cost to complete. The electrical work was almost done and our contractor said that we should come in at or below our budget of $15,000. Two weeks later we got a bill from the electrician for $65,000 and that didn't include any fixtures.

Rod: I was absolutely furious. We sued the contractor and the electrician and they countersued. We had an agonizing jury trial and we lost. But it resulted in the second and third of Porter's laws: "Never hire anyone who looks like a preppy to do anything important" and "Stay clear of jury trials if you're wealthy or prominent." The second law was to be reinforced again later in the Washington Bike Lawsuit. Through it all Diana remained a good friend, although she converted from architecture to sculpture. (A sculptor doesn't have to deal with contractors — or lawyers.)

Georgia: *At the Middleburg branch I hired Holly Hoopes, a local realtor, to be the residential mortgage originator for Middleburg. Her sister had married an old friend of Rod's from Chemical Bank in New York and we'd gone to their wedding. Holly knew everyone in Middleburg and turned out to be a very productive originator. For a number of years we owned the market around Middleburg for the residential mortgage business, until other banks caught on.*

Shortly thereafter Rod met a United Airlines pilot who was investing in and around Middleburg in a variety of deals. Rod introduced me to the pilot and he told me that he knew an excellent loan officer at a bank in Warrenton. Her name was Linda Sandridge.

Linda is a totally self-made person. She started work as a bank teller when she was just out of high school, worked her way up to the accounting department and ultimately up to construction loan officer. According to Linda, when I first met her I said, "You dress well; I like that." She still dresses well.

I hired Linda to be our Middleburg Branch Manager in 1989. She had never been a branch manager but she told me she was sure she could do it. I learned that Linda was able to do anything I asked her to with little or no direction. She has a way with customers that is uncanny. She gets better pricing than anyone else and the customers believe they got a deal. Over the next 15 years she was to have her share of problem credits and she handled them with tough love, bringing them back to health when there was a grain of hope — and being firm with them while minimizing our losses when there was none. She was a great business developer, given her charm combined with an advanced capacity for B.S. (not a Bachelor of Science, but just as good). Under Linda's leadership the Middleburg office flourished. With persistence and charm she lured most of the small businesses in Middleburg away from the other banks.

Middleburg is a funny place. It is divided between really, really rich people with brand names for last names and people who pretend they are really, really rich. Linda called the latter category "Middleburg Wannabees" and there were dozens of them. One was a guy who moved to Middleburg with his girlfriend from California and founded an insurance agency. He opened his accounts with us and insisted that he meet me. He wanted to make sure we could handle all kinds of wires and funds transfers. He bought a huge home in Middleburg and his girlfriend bought a smaller one and they invited everyone to a large catered party at the Virginia Gold Cup. We made a loan on the girlfriend's house but not on his. A couple months later he requested a line of credit of $200,000 for his company. We never extended it because he didn't have anything to offer as collateral and couldn't explain why he needed it. About a year after he arrived, he and his girlfriend disappeared, leaving town with a lot of debt owed to the local merchants. The girlfriend made her mortgage payments for a couple of months, but we finally had to foreclose. It was one of our first REO's (Real Estate Owned as a result of foreclosure). Bankers hate having them — at least this one did. You try to be upbeat because you've convinced yourself that you're adequately covered and the bank isn't going to lose any money, but then you're there on the courthouse steps and an auctioneer reads all the verbiage and asks for bids. I bid on behalf of Southern Financial. We had a second trust of $250,000 over a first trust of $500,000. I naively thought there would be other bidders, but I was the first and only one. Suddenly, we were the proud owners of a strange looking house in Berryville with a price tag of $750,000. We were responsible for insurance, utilities, etc., which was also costing us money. We had to sell the house quickly. Fortunately, two gay guys fell in love with it and bought it from us at a break-even price.

After this episode, I never really put much value in second trusts when they're behind a large first trust. Never look at them as a source of repayment. Take them as additional collateral, but don't delude yourself that is how you are going to be repaid.

There were to be a lot of other Middleburg Wannabees in the ensuing years who made comments like:

"Why do you need a financial statement? The other banks don't."

"I never give my tax returns to a bank."

"The bank down the street didn't trust me and I want a small bank that can be creative."

My last Middleburg story is about a famous jump jockey and trainer whom Rod and I met early on at a cocktail party. He was gorgeous — and very short! I gave him my card. I told him we'd love to have his business. He was in the process of trying to buy some land in Middleburg and I referred him to Linda at the local Southern Financial branch. He called Linda and she thought he was as attractive as I did. She nicknamed him "Blue Eyes." We lent him the money to buy his land and for about the first year everything was fine. But then he started having problems making his payments on time. Linda and I would meet with him and hear his tale of woe. We'd always intend to be hard on him, but we couldn't. He was on our classified/past due list longer than any other borrower ever was. (Rod *yelled at us and pointed out that he was short. Linda said that wouldn't matter if she could get him horizontal.) Blue Eyes always paid when we threatened foreclosure and he ultimately paid off the loan.*

Despite the flake, we did tons of great business in Middleburg. We turned down a lot of loans, but we also issued a lot. We still live there and most of the wannabees have moved on to other venues.

Linda told me from the time I first interviewed her that we should start offering "Harry Homeowner" construction loans, not only in Middleburg but all over Loudoun and Fauquier counties. I'd never heard the phrase before. (**Rod:** It's not a technical term. Linda made it up!) *But after a time we offered construction loans to owner/builders and cornered the market in Fauquier and Loudoun counties. She set up a mini-construction lending department in Middleburg, which until Provident took over serviced all the construction loans throughout the Southern Financial system. We minimized the use of lawyers and tried to do everything internally and our loan losses were almost zero. Ultimately, the expertise we developed in residential construction lending led the way to the construction lending that we started doing for the Money Store's SBA loan program. We soon started doing the SBA loans ourselves and the small business lending, which evolved from the SBA construction loans and became a cornerstone of our strategy five or six years later.*

Rod: Linda is self-taught. She's the best-read person I've ever met. She knows absolutely everything, and if she doesn't, she bullshits. The only thing she didn't read was *Life of Boswell*, which I loved and recommended to her and which Georgia hated.

I pushed it on her too much. If Georgia had read Boswell's *Life of Johnson* and Johnson's *Tour of the Hebrides* before she tried *Life of Boswell*, she'd have loved it. I'm still working on her. Georgia is hopeless. She still reads Danielle Steele.

Georgia: *Linda evolved over time into my clone. She could handle problem customers; she could communicate the toughest messages in a velvet pouch. It wasn't easy for her, but she was marvelous at it. She had spine.*

For Love and Money

Rod: Later in 1987 we had a wrenching personal crisis. My son Devon, who Georgia saw as her own son, had been flying down to Virginia for one weekend a month to stay with us on the farm. One Sunday night he burst into tears and told us he wanted to live with us full time. We had a serious discussion and told him that we'd love to have him stay, but that it would be extraordinarily difficult and emotional. He was just a 10-year-old, but he was adamant. After he returned to Connecticut we arranged for him to be interviewed by our personal attorney, Paul Johnson, and a family law specialist in Paul's firm — without us present. Paul reported back to us that Devon seemed absolutely determined to go ahead. We began the process, which, although ultimately successful, was so traumatic for the three of us that it generated a horror of the judicial process and antipathy for lawyers.

Paul, a gentleman, friend and graduate of Harvard Law School, represented Georgia and I. Devon had a court appointed lawyer, Warner de Puy, from a serious Stamford law firm. My charming former wife, Kathy, had a lawyer from the mold that a friend suggested I get: "Somebody ethnic, with nose hair."

The proceedings went on for months. There was a court appointed social worker and a court appointed psychiatrist, Dr. Kruger, in Westport, Connecticut. Kathy had her own psychiatrist and also told Devon that if he ever came to live with us she would never talk to him again.

We periodically assembled our team for hearings at incredible cost. We flew to Connecticut and "nose hair" filed motions that immediately sent everyone home.

Finally, I was at work one morning and I got a call from Warner. He said he'd gotten a call from Kathy's boyfriend who had talked to Devon, and Warner said that Devon didn't want to come and live with us anymore. It was a kick in the stomach.

I called Georgia. Her response defined her best and was one of the things I love her for other than sex. She said, "Bullshit. Something's wrong; let's go talk to Devon. I'll meet you at National Airport in an hour." We flew to New York, rented a car and drove to Rowayton, Connecticut. To this day it's the only time

Georgia has ever gone anywhere without a complete wardrobe. We got to Rowayton and picked up Devon as he left his school.

At that point we were guilty of kidnapping.

We found out from Devon what had happened. Kathy faked suicide attempts, making sure my oldest son Trent and my daughter Vanessa knew about them. Kathy also told Devon through her boyfriend that she would kill herself if he came to live with us.

We found a pay phone on the Post Road in Darien, Connecticut, called our attorney Paul and asked him to conference in the other two attorneys. We told the three of them where we were and that we were going to Dr. Kruger's office in Westport. If they wanted to have the State Police there we'd turn ourselves in. Dr. Kruger, thank God, was there when we got to Westport and took Devon alone into his office.

After an hour Dr. Kruger came out and told us that it was over. He said that if the attorneys didn't settle immediately and grant us custody that he would inform the state that Devon was being emotionally abused and place him in a foster home. With great anxiety we found a hotel room in Westport that night. The next morning Kathy and her team caved. Devon has been with Georgia and I ever since. Kathy maintained contact and visitations with him for several years, but hasn't really talked to him for a decade. That has to be difficult for Devon.

Georgia: *Devon has been with us since Southern Financial was a year old. Despite their difference in years Devon was engaged to Linda Sandridge for many years. At one Christmas Party, when Devon was 13, and Linda was somewhat older, Devon and Linda danced several dances and Devon asked Linda if she would marry him. She agreed and they were engaged!*

He worked part time in the summers. He was our bookie at the Middleburg Spring Races for years since he was too young to be arrested. And he joined the Bank right after he graduated from college. His blood runs Southern Financial blue.

Growing up, Devon had the typical problems of an adolescent kid. At first we sent him to the public school in Marshall, Virginia, just a couple of miles from the farm. Then there was the vodka incident.

I'll never forget that one. The Principal of Devon's school called me at work and asked me to come to meet in his office immediately. I asked him what was wrong and he said he needed to talk to me. I was annoyed and said that I would rather come tomorrow. He suggested that today would be better. I left the office, which was still in Herndon, and drove the hour to Devon's school. I was nervous and imagining all sorts of terrible things.

I walked into the Principal's office and saw that he had a navy blue canvas bag on his desk with "DEVON" embroidered on it in two inch letters. I'd given it to Devon for Christmas. The Principal told me that someone had found the bag in the bushes with a bottle of vodka in it. I immediately took Devon's side and said someone must have set him up. I asked him how he knew Devon bought it. He suggested we bring Devon in. As Devon arrived the Principal put the bottle of vodka on his desk. At that point I knew our goose was cooked. It was a bottle of Finlandia vodka with a State Wines and Liquors tag. Every Christmas on the way back from New York we stopped at State Wines and Liquors in Delaware and bought several cases of wine and stocked up on high quality vodkas. This was probably the only bottle of Finlandia vodka in our end of Fauquier County. It was almost certainly the only one with a State Wines and Liquors label.

Devon tried to say it wasn't his, but I shut him up. I asked the Principal what our options were. He told us that if Devon decided to leave the school and attend another one that he wouldn't have to report the incident to the authorities and it would never go on his record. (**Rod:** Devon's 12 and Georgia's already plea bargaining on his behalf!) *I told him we'd think about it and get back to him in the morning. I've been forever grateful to that Principal, but I've never bought anyone anything again with their name embroidered on it.*

For Devon's next school we chose Wakefield, which had some warts but overall was excellent. Devon had a great time there and got an incredible education. It was, however, the end of his sports career, such as it was. Wakefield was no Notre Dame. It wasn't even Williams, athletically. At Wakefield, Devon was one of their best athletes, which was cause for concern in and of itself. He played soccer, volleyball, and tennis, and for all three of those sports, he never won a game. Devon came home from soccer games and we asked, "Did you win?" After saying "no" enough times, Devon said, "You know, that's a very negative question, and I always have to give a depressing answer." After that, we asked, "Did you come in second?" Devon then happily responded, "Yes!" (The highlight of Devon's sporting career was a tie in a game against another school's junior varsity team.)

Devon started a band when he was at Wakefield, which practiced first in the house and later in a small barn overlooking the pool, which he and his friends dubbed "The Studio." They performed around Warrenton and actually met and spent time with several members of The Dave Matthews Band in Charlottesville. That all came to an end when Devon's girlfriend ran away with his group's guitar player. If Devon had continued hanging out with Dave Matthews, Rod and I possibly could have retired much earlier, but it was not to be.

Devon got into James Madison University in Harrisonburg, Virginia, which is a superb school that he enjoyed a little too much. At the end of his first semester, he and I had a serious sit-down. I kept it from Rod until I couldn't any longer.

His grades were awful. He was on academic probation and told me he didn't want to finish college. He said he wanted to do things with his hands, like blow glass pipes. I said that would be fine, but he would first have to complete the next semester. I told him that he would have to pay for whatever he wanted to do and he agreed. He said that he wanted to go to Costa Rica for six months. I said that would be fine.

Rod: They'd already worked it out by the time I got home, but they let me feel like I was part of the pact.

Georgia: As it turned out, it was the best thing Devon ever did. He made the Dean's List his second semester.

When he got back that summer he was skinny as a rail. He had long flowing hair and two earrings. Rod always told him that if he got an earring that Rod would cut off his ear. With two pierced ears, Rod lost.

Devon needed to earn some money to finance his trip to Costa Rica. He applied for a job at the Red Fox Inn & Tavern in Middleburg. Turner Reuter, Rod's friend who owned the Red Fox, told Devon that he could either cut his hair or wear it in a pony tail with a hair net after he sprayed it. Devon agreed to the pony tail and for a long time kept the hairspray in his car. He eventually tired of that, started worrying about "split ends," he said, and got a haircut. Now, with short hair and no earrings he looks like his father's son.

He earned a ton of money working at the Red Fox. It was a great experience for him. He made some close friends and learned that work is work. After six months he went to Costa Rica and had the wonderful time he'd promised himself and of which we all were envious. When he came back we sent him to Buenos Aires, Argentina, where we'd arranged an internship. He only lasted three weeks. He got mononucleosis, complicated by partying all night, which we thought was hepatitis and decided to bring him back.

When he returned he finished up at James Madison — more or less on time.

Rod: When Devon graduated from James Madison he came on board with Southern Financial. He knew everyone in the bank. We put him on the Merchant Services business where we'd been having problems. It was a business where we weren't making any money and our customers hated us. We wanted our customers to use us, but our third-party provider was awful. We plunked Devon into the business reporting to Michelle Buckles, who had been with us forever and had done everything. We ordered them to fix it and Devon and Michelle did.

Devon was a junior banker. However, he was the Prince of Southern Financial. It was an extraordinarily difficult, but important, role to play that few people could have taken on. Everyone could have hated him for what he was, but over the next several years he built his own constituency. He had his people and we had ours. By the time we sold it was not clear whose constituency was more important.

Georgia: Devon blossomed at the Bank. He worked hard and everyone knew it. He has a wonderful personality and makes people laugh. There's no one in the Bank who doesn't like him — even if they don't like Rod and me.

Rod: Over time we added more and more products to Commercial Services. ACH Cash Manager, then ARTS/WebLockBox and, finally, Southern Cash Manager. It was Devon's job to implement the products that Aidan and Jacques Smith developed. It became the core of our competitive edge. It was ultimately a very important contributor to Southern's earnings and ultimate success. The Commercial Services Department was ultimately critically important for what the bank was to become.

FIRREA AND OUR CONVERSION TO A COMMERCIAL BANK

Georgia: Telling Devon's story has gotten us way ahead of ourselves.

It's 1989 and Congress has passed FIRREA. Rod got a summary of the legislation and called me one night with one of his bright ideas: "FIRREA specifically allows strong thrifts to convert to commercial bank charters." The thrifts, once converted, would still be covered by FSLIC insurance, but in every other way they would become commercial banks. Rod said, "Why don't we become the first thrift to convert?" His excitement was contagious. We could escape the morass and the negativism of the thrift industry. But it wasn't that easy. The dying bureaucracy of the thrift industry didn't want to let the healthy thrifts go.

We began to work with our law firm at the time, Silver Friedman and Taff, and submitted an application to the OTS to be allowed to exit their realm. We sent another application to the OCC to enter theirs. The OCC responded, saying that they would have to come in to the Bank and conduct a full regulatory exam. Exams paralyze small banks, but about 10 OCC examiners descended on little Southern Financial. They stayed about three weeks. They pulled all of our credit files, all of our reconciliations and interviewed all of our loan officers. They told us that if we were to receive a National Bank Charter, we'd have to rewrite all of our policies. With my best Westchester Country Club smile I told them that we would be happy to comply with all of their requirements.

We got conditional approval to become a commercial bank with a national charter. Post FIRREA we were the first in the country. We were on a high.

We then had to submit our conditional approval back to the OTS and wait ... and wait some more. The OTS ultimately had no interest whatsoever in approving our conversion, even though FIRREA had specifically approved such conversions. In essence, we were a captive fee-paying client and if they approved the conversion they were going to lose a profitable client. Their client base was dwindling and they certainly didn't want to accelerate the process.

Our lawyers kept bugging the OTS. About nine months after we received our conditional approval from the OCC, the OTS finally said OK. We went back to the OCC and they told us that because nearly a year had passed since their last exam they would have to conduct another one. They also told us we'd have to pay for the exam again. I was distraught. I asked them for an estimate of how much it would cost. They said they didn't know because we'd grown since the last exam, which also meant it would take longer than the last one. I asked whether they could give me a maximum amount and they said no.

By that time we had spent $75,000 in legal fees; $25,000 to apply and $20,000 on the last exam. This all also demanded a ton of management time. What if they really didn't want to approve any thrifts to become commercial banks? I certainly didn't want to be a test case. It was clearly the public policy of the United States to foster conversions. It was enshrined in FIRREA. It was less clear that the bureaucracy wanted it to happen. The OTS didn't want to let us out. Maybe the OCC didn't want to let us in. I couldn't take the chance.

I went back to the Board and explained the situation and recommended we pull our application. The Bank simply couldn't handle another exam, particularly since we couldn't pin the OCC down as to how much it would cost. The Board agreed. We learned a lesson. Don't try to be the first to do anything that involves regulatory approval. I'm not sure there were ever any conversions.

Some five years later we finally changed our charter, but to a Virginia state charter. It was a much smoother process and we left the thrift industry behind forever.

Branch Purchases

In early 1990 I received a call from Dave Campbell, then the President of Ameribanc, asking whether Southern would like to purchase two of their branches. Ameribanc was a large thrift that was just holding on and desperately needed to bolster their capital. I talked to Rod and his immediate response was that we have to have them. So Bill Lagos and I visited both locations. One was in Leesburg, where we really wanted to be, and the other was in Warrenton. Bill and I loved the Leesburg location, but did not think the Warrenton location made sense for us. When I told Rod, he said buy the Leesburg branch, but just buy the Warrenton deposits and transfer them to Southern Financial's existing location in Warrenton. What an idea! I got back to Dave and started to negotiate. We finally agreed on a deposit premium of 1.25% and a small amount for the fixed assets. If it wasn't the best deal done in the early 1990s, it was close. The only problem was that it spoiled us when we bid for other branches once the RTC started selling. In Northern Virginia they went for 4% to 12% and we were always the underbidder. We didn't win a single one. Crestar and George Mason Bank won many of them and built themselves into serious institutions before selling out. In retrospect we should have bid more aggressively, but we have no regrets. At the price we got them the Ameribanc branches were a bonanza.

It was the first time we'd ever implemented a major project and the way we did it was to define our culture until the end. It became the epitome of multitasking. We wrote a letter to all of the Ameribanc depositors, internally without an outside agency. We designed envelopes with welcome balloons. We printed the letters. Our own people stuffed them in envelopes during business hours and Billy borrowed a dolly to take them to the Post Office. Our one extravagance was to hire a part-timer to help us. She proved to be so slow we told her not to come back the next day.

The Ameribanc transaction doubled our deposit base in Warrenton and added a $15 million branch in Leesburg in one weekend. We were on our way and the confidence that this transaction engendered was the basis for Southern's "can-do" attitude until the end. (**Rod:** No, again, it originated with Georgia.)

The following year Bill Lagos got a call from one of our landlords telling him he had a location for a branch with all the furniture and equipment already in place. The rent wasn't bad, but we would have to negotiate with the RTC on the fixed assets. Billy and I went to look. It was a good location in Fairfax City, Virginia, in a fairly upscale mini-shopping area. We'd be moving in closer to the inner suburbs. We discussed it at length with our Board at our next meeting and it was agreed that this was probably the time to take a stab at Fairfax.

Billy and I set up a meeting with a representative from the RTC at the branch. The inside of the branch was beautiful — big brass chandeliers, a walk-in vault, eight mahogany desks, a couch and a sitting area. It was the most nicely decorated branch we had.

The representative from the RTC was very formal. He said that he had gotten appraisals on everything and that we would have to pay the appraised value. Billy and I were a bit intimidated, but we said fine. I knew our cheapest branches had cost $100,000 minimum to equip and build out. I tried to sneak a look at the bottom line on his sheet and thought I saw $160,000. When I asked him how much, he said, "I must get $16,000 for everything." Billy and I looked at each other and said OK. It was a steal. The desks alone would have cost $1,500 each. It was our government at work.

We were able to open quite quickly, though admittedly, the branch location wasn't the greatest. In 1996 we bought a much better branch in the heart of Fairfax City and transferred all of our deposits — and the beautiful desks — there.

THE MR. BEASLEY STORY

The Mr. Beasley story became an integral part of Southern Financial lore because it illustrated many important things about our culture and how it differed from the world around us.

George Beasley was a loan officer we hired in the early 1990s and was with us for only a couple of weeks. He told us that he had great contacts in Northern Virginia and could bring in a huge volume of loans. He was about 50 and had spent his whole career in banking in the Fairfax area.

Ground Game

At that time all of the loan officers reported directly to me. There were no secretaries or assistants. Each loan officer prepared their loan submissions. All five of the loan officers met with me weekly in my office to discuss the status of all of the loans in progress as well as any new loans that were being proposed.

We had a policy that if the volume of loans closed in a quarter did not reach the agreed target, no one in the Commercial Loan Department would get a bonus. People who didn't perform didn't get bonuses, but, worse, a non-performer hurt everyone. That intentionally put peer pressure on all of the laggards. As a result the Commercial Loan Department never missed its target.

My weekly meetings never went very long. We never had time to philosophize. For me it's let's get it done — now!

The last meeting that George Beasley attended was coming to an end. I noticed that George hadn't said much and his loans in process weren't going anywhere. I asked him why and he said he was working on them. I told him, "I want that loan proposal on my desk by the end of the day and the other by the end of the week." He nodded, but kept looking at Linda, who was sitting beside him. I said that I wouldn't take any excuses. He'd been sitting on the loan far too long. It wasn't doing the Bank or the customer any good. The meeting ended and everyone dispersed.

About 15 minutes later Linda reappeared in my office. She said, "I'm not sure George is going to make it." After the meeting he asked Linda to come into his office. George then told her, "I've got something to tell you my friend. I can't type!" Linda told him not to worry; anyone can type with two fingers. She said she'd help him make corrections. Then George said, "Linda, remember the good old days when you could hand your handwritten draft to a secretary who would type everything up?" Linda answered as only Linda could, saying, "No, George, I don't. I was the secretary you men handed the draft to!" Linda tried to reassure him that he could do it and that she'd help him as much as he needed. She seemed concerned and I said to keep me posted.

At about 2:30 pm someone from the branch called me and asked if I knew where George was. George's office was adjacent to the branch and he had several messages, but no one knew when he was supposed to return to the office. I asked Linda if she knew his whereabouts. She said that at about noon he'd told her he was going out for a cheeseburger. A little later she checked his office. It was totally cleaned out except for the Bank's pager. We never heard from him again.

About a month later he tried to collect unemployment insurance. Linda told the woman who called us about the unemployment insurance claim that we never fired him. He'd simply gone out for a cheeseburger and never returned. She laughed and needless to say he never collected.

The big joke at Southern from then on was that you could go out for a hamburger, but cheeseburgers were forbidden.

Going Public

Rod: We always knew we were going to have to go public if we were going to grow into a serious institution. I started pushing Georgia and talking about it with the Board in 1990-91, but the S&L crisis was in full swing. The RTC was closing more S&Ls every week. We'd read the IDC book every quarter and try to figure out who would be next. I was then with Greenwich Capital and we won the contract with the RTC on how to securitize the problem loans they owned from the S&Ls they took over. This was when Madison Savings and Loan in Little Rock, Arkansas, went down. Hillary Clinton was inextricably entwined with the company, as well as Jim MacDougall, despite all of the subsequent denials and stonewalling. They've never issued a compilation, but I believe that Madison set some kind of a record in terms of losses to the taxpayers as a multiple of its capital. Madison was on a smaller scale than Lincoln — the Keating Five scandal — and some of the other big ones, but it was a case of massive incompetence and fraud, which was to become an all too familiar pattern.

Our problem was that we were tarred by the Madison brush. We were doing fine in a sea of red ink. We'd avoided the traps that so many, but not all, of the S&Ls so gleefully found. We made money every month from the second month we were open. By 1992 our earnings were so strong and consistent that we started paying dividends. That really felt good.

So what to do? We talked to a lot of investment bankers and there was no shot at us doing an offering at or above our book value. (Though they were the same investment bankers who took the dotcoms public at insane multiples during the bubble, just before they went under.) That killed me. Georgia had built an institution that had made money every month of its existence while everything around her was going under, and yet somehow it wasn't worth its equity value? I learned that apparently many investment bankers aren't really very smart (even though I was one, too). They flow along with the tide. They can do spreadsheets and comps, but they really understand very little.

It was an awful low point for us. Georgia had worked so hard and the Bank was performing brilliantly. We were full steam ahead in a sea of foundering institutions and we couldn't get anyone to notice.

Jefferson Savings and Loan — the big thrift in Warrenton where we'd moved our headquarters — was on an extended swan dive to oblivion. Among other things they had a portfolio of loans in the southwest. The other Warrenton thrift, Liberty S&L, eventually proved to be even worse.

Jefferson eventually organized a private equity offering for enough money to keep themselves alive until they could sell the franchise to a commercial bank. I was amazed and envious. I called National Capital Companies, who had done the deal. It was a three- or four-person company. The key guy was Louis Mayberg, who lived in Georgetown. I was frank with Louis. "If you can do an offering for a carcass like Jefferson you can certainly do one for us," I said.

Louis and Steve Clinton came and spent time with us. (Steve Clinton ultimately left National Capital and we worked with him on the First Savings Bank acquisition years later. Louis went quiet and we haven't heard from him in years.) They ultimately did our offering, raising us $5 million at a price just over book. It was a very important step for us. We were now a public company. Our ticker symbol was to be SFFB until the end.

Problem Credits

Georgia: *Before we move on to the Passing Game I need to tell you about some of our difficult credits. People think that all banks do is take people's money. I can't tell you how many people have told me, "Do you know how much you've made from me this year? Over $100,000." Banks pay for their deposits and their other sources of funding. Even when they don't they provide services to customers that are very expensive. We provided "Totally Free Checking" to our customers from the beginning. "Totally Free Checking" is just what it says it is. Free. But the money that the bank has to lend in those accounts is expensive to the bank because of the cost of the services it has to provide.*

It's not easy to be a good banker. It's easier to say no, or it's easier to be formulaic or policy driven. A lot of banks will make a bad loan in a given sector and then decide that they won't make any more loans in that sector. Lots of banks won't work with restaurants or telecommunications companies or hotels. That's a lot easier than trying to figure out where you went wrong the first time, or trying to figure out how to structure a good loan to a company in the sector.

When we went through credit training at Chemical they told us that there are three "C's" in credit. The first is "Character." I was to learn over and over again how important that is. Here's one example:

We were approached in Warrenton by a guy who had an existing, ostensibly successful business in California that he'd inherited from his father. He was moving to Warrenton to start another company in a related business. After looking carefully at his financials and discussing his projections we lent him much of the money he needed to start the new company. He had kept his house in California, although he had moved to Warrenton. He gave us some excuse as to why he couldn't give us a second trust on the California house. We thought we were smart and got the California company to guarantee our loan to the new Virginia company. Everything seemed to go well for a time. He was a deacon or an elder in one of the local churches, and he came to our yearly party at the Middleburg Spring Races twice. He was an excellent amateur photographer and took pictures of all of the guests.

But one day he came into my office and told me that he was liquidating the company in California. I asked him why. He said it wasn't doing well. I asked about the company's debt to its California lenders. He said nonchalantly that he didn't have the money to pay them. I said, "Banks don't like it when you don't pay other banks." He said, "Don't worry, we'll pay Southern Financial." From then on, I didn't trust him, but it was too late.

About a year later he came in and told us that he was closing his operation in Warrenton. It was a shock. We'd been monitoring the company closely and had several emotional discussions with our borrower. The company had hit a rough patch, but over the years we'd nursed a lot of companies with a lot bigger problems back to health. This borrower, however, decided to throw in the towel — exactly like he did in California. There, he tried to strip as much cash out of the company as he could. We suspected that he took a lot of equipment out of the California company, sold some and brought the rest to Virginia.

Rod: We had personal guarantees, perfected liens on receivables and perfected liens on the company's equipment, and a second trust on his factory. Our borrower shortly went personally bankrupt so we couldn't attach his personal assets. Then he went on a full court press to grab as much cash from the company as possible. He collected the mail and deposited the checks from the company's receivables in another bank. He tried to sell the factory building in a way that would have given him cash and left no money to cover our second trust. He then tried to sell the company's equipment. Again, this was the deacon who'd come to our parties. We'd talked about going fly fishing together.

We finally hired a guard and locked the whole thing down. We collected the checks; we told him that if he didn't give us the money from the other collections from the other receivables we'd have him arrested. We stopped the insider sale of his factory. But most importantly I learned how much equity he had in his Boston Digimatics and intervened just before he could sell them to a foreign buyer. I still don't know what Boston Digimatics do, but they're two stories tall, have a lot of levers and gears, and are the kind of thing any guy would want in his workshop. More importantly, people are willing to pay hundreds of thousands of dollars for one.

We ended up losing a couple of hundred thousand dollars on this loan, but could have lost much more. More importantly it was a lesson: there's no substitute for character and honesty. If your borrower doesn't have those traits there's no way to help them.

Georgia: *Bankers who say they never make bad loans miss lots of good ones. When you're a banker it's inevitable that you give loans to ventures that just don't make it. It's just reality. You take your lumps and go on to the next deal. Lending is inherently risky and making a good loan takes time and effort before and after you advance money to the borrower. It was the work with the customer* after *the loan was made that set Southern Financial apart from other lenders. Our commercial lending officers worked with our customers* after *they made the loan. We worked with our customers. Like me, they weren't easy, but they knew we were on their team and if they got in trouble that we'd do anything we could to help them. Other banks will call or not renew a loan as soon as a company falters. We spent hours with our borrowers. We gave them advice. We helped them with their accounting. We helped them make the tough decisions. If it was feasible we lent them more money. I'd tell the commercial lending officer to come up with alternatives, with a new proposal. We were tough, but we wanted our customers to succeed. Some didn't, but it wasn't because we hadn't exhausted all the alternatives. For many of our customers who made it, we like to think that if they'd been with another bank the outcome would have been different.*

We had tons of success stories that we loved. One of our most profound successes was one of our most high-maintenance customers — and he would admit it! He was a very successful veterinarian in Northern Virginia who came to us with the objective of building an absolutely state-of-the-art vet clinic in one of the most upscale communities in the region. (**Rod:** *It's one of the most upscale communities on the east coast. Dick Cheney, my boy, lives nearby.*) *He had traveled throughout the US and looked at everything that had been done before. He'd incorporated every positive idea he'd seen into his own plans. They were great.*

The vet was going to need a lot of money and we agonized over the decision. Finally we decided to go ahead and approve it. Naturally there were cost overruns. (I have yet to see anyone who has not *had cost overruns.) We had factored in a contingency, but he was still short. We lent him some more money and he opened his doors. He was able to rent his old facilities to generate additional cash flow. But he still wound up being tight and he panicked. The vet came into the Bank several times and threatened to file bankruptcy. I told him to calm down.*

He kept asking for more money. He told me and the loan officer that he needed "a candy jar full of money just in case." This was a guy on the brink of fantastic success. I know this because, today, he is as rich as we are. But he could barely cope with the perceived uncertainty at the time.

The vet hired some advisor to tell him how to get out of his hole. (He wasn't in one!) The advisor said that maybe he should file bankruptcy. (The business was cash flow positive!) Not only is he right, he's still our friend. We love the vet, but he wasn't a great financial guy.

A lot of our borrowers weren't financial experts. They were honest entrepreneurs, who were trying to build their businesses. They weren't doing it for charity. They were doing it for themselves and their families.

John Chang and Washington Bike

Georgia: *Ironically our biggest disaster was a loan we never completed because it was to a venture that we knew early on didn't have a chance.*

John Chang was an early customer of our Herndon branch. From one bicycle store he built a small chain of stores in Northern Virginia. He was a Korean immigrant and our previous experience with folks like him had been excellent. He was primarily a depositor, but we had extended his company a small line of credit that was rarely used.

John approached us for a loan to purchase some land in Manassas along Route 66 where he wanted to build a velodrome, which is a bicycle park. Initially it was pitched as just a very large bicycle store, but it grew in his mind into something else. We eventually learned that it had become "his dream."

We processed John's application and approved a first trust of $1.5 million and an SBA loan of $1.0 million that would have a second trust on the property. The *approval was subject to a satisfactory appraisal of the project as completed as well as construction plans and contracts. John had a contract to buy the land and had to close fairly quickly, so we extended a loan with a first trust to permit him to close on the land.*

By this time we had closed over 100 SBA loans, and allowing a borrower to purchase the land before construction plans were complete was fairly common. Several months went by and John finally came in with new plans. To our amazement and consternation the total cost of the project had increased from $2.5 million to $9.5 million. I was told about it by a colleague and my reaction was, "This is ridiculous. Tell him no way." Keep in mind that at the time we had around $20 million in capital and a legal lending limit of around $3 million. We could not legally make the loan. Linda told John that we would help him explore his options, but first he had to get his arms around the project. It had spiraled out of control. He told Linda that he had sponsors who would pay part of the costs. Linda subsequently talked to one of the supposed sponsors who told Linda that the project was not doable. Still, he came back with a second set of cost estimates for $7.5 million. That was still not viable, at least not for us.

At that point I met with John and told him there was no way we could finance such a large undertaking. We learned he'd begun construction, which was in contravention of his loan agreement. I told him to stop. We told John that we weren't going to lend him any more money because the costs were so far out of line with the original loan request. At that point he started to sob and then told us not to tell anyone that he "cry like baby." (When he got upset his English worsened.) John said for the first, but not the last time, that I had destroyed "his dream." (**Rod:** Porter's fourth law: Never, ever finance anyone's dream. Let them finance it.)

I left the meeting convinced John was crazy, but felt sorry for him. I told Linda to check with the potential sponsors and then she and I would approach the Flory Group, a not-for-profit that helps small businesses get started, to see if they had any ideas for how to assist him. The next day we met with Linda Decker and Karen Talak of Flory. He had already been there. They agreed that the project had gotten too grandiose, but they would look for some government program that could help.

We emphasized that he needed to stop construction until he got financing. We left thinking we'd done everything we could do.

John continued to build and we got construction draw requests that we turned down, including a large one from Bays Construction. Lynn Bays had briefly been a Director of Southern Financial. To this day I am amazed she started such a large project without verifying that John had enough funding to complete the construction.

John continued to build without any hope of getting financing. I worried that we would get mechanics liens on our land where we held the first lien. So we froze all of his money and sent him a demand letter. He came in screaming that we release his funds and we ultimately did. (Years later at the trial we learned that it wasn't his money, but it didn't help.)

The construction finally stopped. He told us he was going to sue us and he did.

I can't tell you how many times I passed that unfinished building on Rt. 66 in Manassas and get sick to my stomach. He ultimately found a lawyer by the name of Lorenzo Bean. Lorenzo was famous at the time. He'd represented the owner of a golf driving range who'd refused to plant as many trees on the berm as the county wanted to hide the driving range from the road. The owner ultimately went to jail. (I don't ever recall hearing about anyone else going to jail for not planting trees.)

With John Chang, Lorenzo thought he'd won the lottery. He sued Southern Financial for $90 million. I thought it was a nuisance lawsuit.

We hired Tom Gorman, whom we'd used for years for litigation and bankruptcy matters. Tom was a reasonable lawyer who didn't run up the clock. Lorenzo, unfortunately, was a clown who didn't have anything else to do except run up the clock. Lorenzo started discovery and it took our people days. I spent over eight hours with him and nearly went crazy. The process took more than a year. Lorenzo got delays and then went to a "non-suit," whatever that was, and then back to a suit. The trial was finally scheduled for a week in July. Unfortunately, it was to be a jury trial.

A week before the trial I met with Tom. He was worried about a jury trial featuring a poor little immigrant against a "big bank," even though we really weren't a "big bank" by any stretch of the imagination at the time. Tom was also worried about John Chang's wife, Hannah. He thought she was a cool cookie. She had a senior job at Freddie Mac. She faked linguistic ignorance and the supportive wife thing.

Tom told me that I would be the only person to sit with him through the whole trial. He said my appearance would be important. With some embarrassment he advised me that I should dress very conservatively. I thought I did. He said dark colors (for chrissakes it was summer) and more importantly no jewelry.

Rod: Those of you who know Georgia know she has a serious penchant for gold and diamonds. She typically wears a slew of rings, a Cartier watch, a bracelet and two gold necklaces. She doesn't feel dressed without her jewelry. The funny thing is that she wears it for herself, not other people.

Georgia: *The trial started with jury selection. We felt confident since the trial was at the Fauquier County Courthouse, two blocks from our headquarters. We hoped we'd have some sympathy as a local bank. The plaintiff was Korean. There were no Korean people who lived or worked in Fauquier County.*

It took a full day to pick the jury. Tom did the picking for our side. The judge was famous and had been called in from semi-retirement to preside over the trial.

From the beginning Lorenzo was his usual buffoonish self. We sensed that the judge didn't buy his act. On the second day Lorenzo began his opening argument, yelling, "Georgia Derrico killed John Chang's dream!" It was a theme we were to hear over and over during the coming days. They made it the centerpiece of their strategy.

He then put John Chang on the stand. John said, "Georgia Derrico killed my dream," and started crying.

We never answered that accusation because it was so stupid, but I had to sit there and listen to it without my jewelry. There is no law that requires banks to finance anyone's dream. I've got a lot of dreams, but I know if I want to fulfill them it's my responsibility.

The proper response to Lorenzo and John's claims would have been, "You assholes, we were willing to finance a $2.5 million project. You didn't have the wherewithal to build anything costing one dime more than that. No one else in their right mind would even contemplate it. We couldn't legally have lent you the money, but even if we could have we wouldn't have. We saved you from disaster." (P.S. John Chang didn't lose any money. He sold the project and paid everyone off.)

We should have said that but we didn't. The next several days were the worst of my life. The only high points were when the judge reprimanded Lorenzo.

One day they had an old bank examiner flown in from the Midwest to testify that when we froze John's assets to get him to stop construction we were in violation of Federal Reserve regulations. Tom told me then that "expert witnesses" are "whores." If you have a job with an impressive title and no conscience being an expert witness is an easy way to make a living forever after you retire. It's the ultimate "pay for say" job. (Pardon me if I sound bitter.)

Tom and I couldn't read the jury at all. Lorenzo took so much time that by the fourth day we hadn't called any of our witnesses. We thought that Lorenzo must have alienated the jury by taking so long. Tom decided to be quick, but thorough when we began again the next week.

I was sitting in the courtroom every day totally strung out. I went home every night and told Rod I couldn't stand another day. He said that I had to and that the next morning I'd go, sit there and listen to the lies without my jewelry. Linda, Mary Ellen Clancy and Marie Taylor Leibson all testified on Southern Financial's behalf and they were terrific. I'm sure they were all as stressed as I was. This was our life and John Chang and Lorenzo Bean were trying to destroy it.

Both sides finally rested and the jury went into deliberations. Tom stayed at the courthouse and I went back to the office and tried to get back to work.

The following day at 2:00 pm the jury came back. I knew that whatever the verdict would be I'd need time to collect myself so I could address my team. So I'd asked Tom and Rod to meet me at a coffee shop down the block from my office whenever the verdict came in. That day Tom called and Rod and I met him. Tom looked awful when he appeared at the coffee shop. The verdict was worse than our worst nightmare.

We lost on all but one count and, contrary to Virginia law, John Chang was awarded punitive damages. The verdict totaled over $5 million. Given the constraints of Virginia law, which limits punitive damages to $350,000, somehow our penalty was about $2.5 million — an entire year of the Bank's earnings at the time. Tom told us that John Chang had asked to shake the hands of the members of the jury and the judge ignored him. More importantly the judge had not issued a ruling, and the verdict had no legal standing until he did. Tom told us that the judge probably would rule in 60 days or so. Legally we were nowhere until that ruling.

Needless to say, we were devastated. I put on my best face and told my people. They were furious.

We were in legal limbo and weren't sure what to do. The full amount of the verdict was devastating, but we knew we'd never have to pay it all. Fortunately the Warrenton papers were weeklies and we'd have two days to decide what to say. Rod called Steve Joseph of Sandler O'Neill and asked him to come down the next morning. Steve was a friend with mature judgement. He wasn't a lawyer and knew nothing about rural Virginia, which meant he was perfect. We needed someone with a clear head to bounce ideas off of. Our corporate attorney at the time said we should put everything in a detailed press release. Tom said that we shouldn't say anything. The judge hadn't ruled and the punitive damages were all wrong.

Steve, Rod and I sat in Rod's office most of the next day. We knew we had to have a statement by late afternoon. I was incredibly emotional. Rod and I went back and forth on what our statement should be. Steve listened and gave us his input. I don't think I could have handled it without him. In the end we ignored the lawyers and wrote a simple press release ourselves. We stated the facts simply, noted that we were awaiting the judge's ruling and stated that if the judge ruled against us we would appeal the verdict.

The next day the story was all over the local papers and it was a low point for all of us. The women in the local coffee house expressed their sympathy. We got calls from the bank equity analysts who covered our stock. Most were supportive, but Jeff Smith from Sandler O'Neill, who had just started covering us, was very concerned. Finally, Rod was able to convince him that we had just done what any prudent banker should have done to protect the Bank's position. The jury verdict was an aberration.

I was physically and emotionally drained. Carmelita Bernardo, who had been with me from the beginning, came into my office and said, "I've prayed and prayed for us. Don't worry." I almost burst into tears. The trial was over and I was shattered, but at least I could wear my jewelry again.

On a practical level we had no idea how much the verdict would cost the Bank. We would have to report earnings for the third quarter shortly after September 30th, but the judge was expected to rule on October 31st, so we had some time. In the periods before the trial we'd reserved maybe $750,000. That looked like it wouldn't be nearly enough. I don't know how I went on, but I did. I just put it out of my mind as best I could.

On the morning of October 31st Rod and I went to the hospital to have our first colonoscopies. Devon picked us up at 11:00 am since you can't drive as a result of the medication. (You really do feel drunk from it.) I checked my phone messages and Tom Gorman had left a message saying that Judge Robbins had thrown out the jury's verdict in its entirety and ordered a new trial. My reaction was muted since I was sedated. I told Rod that I'd think about it later, but there was no way I was going through another trial. We didn't.

Chapter Three
The Passing Game

The Passing Game

Georgia: I'd hired Dave Campbell in late 1996 to be President of Southern Financial Bank and my number two. After about a year he decided that he wasn't contributing enough and could do more somewhere else. It was an amicable separation. Our paths have crossed many times since and we've always been supportive of each other. So I was left running what was then a $250 million bank singlehandedly. The Board kept telling me that if the Bank is going to grow I needed someone else to take some of the burden off me. The Board was right. I had a very strong middle management team, but there was nobody besides me making major decisions. And considering the growth of the Bank, no single person should have been making all the major decisions. But I also didn't want to damage the fun-loving, entrepreneurial culture I'd created. I didn't want a prima donna who would harm the "can do" attitude that was Southern Financial's main strength.

Separately, Rod bugged me about replacing Dave Campbell. He was pushing me to hire one of our close friends he thought would be excellent as a replacement for Dave, but I just wasn't sure.

I flew from Washington to New York for my Aunt Betty's wake. I was to meet Rod and my entire family at a restaurant on Arthur Avenue, in the Bronx's Little Italy. On the plane I racked my brain, thinking about who I could work with. The thought struck me like a bolt of lightning: how about Rod? At the time he was President of FX Concepts in New York, traveling a lot and commuting to the farm in Virginia on weekends. I loved being with him and working with him. The Bank could afford to pay him a decent salary, though not what he was making at FX Concepts. The problem was how to convince him?

I met Rod on Arthur Avenue before my family arrived — we're both always early — and I couldn't hold in my excitement. I told him that I had found someone who could be President of Southern Financial and that he couldn't say no until he heard me out. It was someone everyone at Southern Financial knew and wouldn't change the Bank's "can do" culture. It was also a person everyone would know was not in *competition with me, and someone who could help me build the Bank into what it could be.* Rod!

His first reaction was "no way." He didn't know the slightest thing about, nor did he have the slightest interest in, retail banking. I told him he could learn, and that I also knew he loved Asset/Liability Management, which he'd been doing at Southern Financial from day one. I knew he loved marketing and was fascinated by technology — areas where I had no interest at all. I told him to think about it before making a decision, and added that if he truly loved me he would say yes. (I play hard when I want something I know is right.)

Rod: No fair!

(See Appendix C – "Interest is Compounded" and Appendix D – "Duo has Expansion Plans")

Other than the commute from Virginia to New York every week, I was having a ball at FX Concepts, which was then and now the world's largest privately owned manager of foreign exchange risk. It's incredibly stimulating to deal with smart people at the top of their game. John Taylor, the Chairman of FX Concepts, is incredibly bright. Our customers were associated with some of the world's most sophisticated entities. I'd brought in as clients The World Bank, John Deere and Siemens to add to a very distinguished roster, which had already included companies like Eastman Kodak and Bell South. I was writing articles about things like heterodacstisity and leptokurtosis, which drive spellcheck crazy. I enjoyed immensely working with my two closest associates, Pike Talbert and Scarlett Mendoza, and the rest of the FX Concepts team. I was traveling all over the world and interfacing with fascinating people. The only cloud on my relationship with FX Concepts was that I had tried to convince John Taylor that the company needed some serious outside capital and that Pike and I would like some serious ownership. John ultimately didn't agree which, in retrospect, I can understand.

I was initially taken aback by Georgia's proposal. On the negative side, I didn't know anything about bank operations. While I love working with people who challenge me, I don't deal well with incompetent or unmotivated people. Georgia will tell you that I just ignore them and that's largely true.

On the positive side, since Georgia moved to Virginia in 1985 I'd had to commute to New York from Virginia every year but two, when I was running my mortgage company. That's a lot of shuttle flights and a lot of nights spent away from Georgia. Moreover, I'd been peripherally involved with Southern Financial as a board member since the beginning and I knew all the people. Finally, unlike FX Concepts, Georgia and I had a very serious investment in Southern Financial. We would have an opportunity, together, to build some serious wealth.

But it really was the commute. I'd have a car pick me up at the farm at 5:00 am on Mondays to take me to National Airport for the 7:00 am shuttle. Sometimes if my car didn't arrive I'd wake Devon up to drive me. If all went well I was in the office at 57th street by 9:00 am, halfway through the company's Monday morning meeting — and a total zombie. I had the same schedule at Morgan Stanley and it was a killer.

Georgia: *During the next couple of weeks Rod called several people he respected and who knew both of us to ask what they thought about the two of us working together. The response was generally quite positive. Dave Booth, a major stockholder and an old friend of Rod's from Morgan Stanley, said it would be a great idea if our marriage could stand it. Devon thought we were crazy. We talked about it a lot and decided that it could work, though, because we respected each other so much. We continued to fight as much as ever on personal issues but not about the Bank.*

Rod then told FX Concepts Chairman John Taylor that he wanted to leave to join Southern Financial. John wished him well. We went on vacation in Italy before Rod started as President of Southern Financial in April 1998.

It worked out better than I could have imagined.

Rod is a man's man. Most men like him immediately. (**Rod:** Most women like me immediately, too!) *He's outgoing, loves to have fun and will talk about anything he finds interesting. Having been involved in the Bank from the beginning he knew all of its strengths and weaknesses. He's so comfortable with* *himself that he never needed to impose his personality on what was there and what was already successful. He never interfered with what was good. At the beginning that was tested over and over. Everyone naturally probed to see if they could exploit any fissures between the two of us. We learned early on that we had to email each other everything, however innocuous. Rod is a bit on the forgetful side. We had candid discussions about things he forgot to tell me.*

Rod understood early on how important the Bank's "can do" culture was to its success, which had been extraordinary. He embraced our culture without reservation.

Rod prides himself on being a business strategist. He is a conceptualizer about trends, events and directions. He will talk to about a half-dozen people who he believes, like him, in thinking outside the box. That's one way he avoided making major mistakes on the portfolio (except the IOs).

Rod's ultimate strength is that he's serenely confident that he can do anything in business. He's played with the best in the world on an equal level and is comfortable dealing with anyone. Some people call it arrogance. My mother Rose sometimes said: "How do you spell 'arrogant'? 'R-O-D.'" But it's not really arrogance with him, just profound self-confidence.

Rod: Georgia got me on board by telling me that I could do the things I liked to do. I guess I assumed that at least I would do what I had always done: the securities portfolio and writing all the prose in the annual report. Georgia would never admit it, but I had always written the prose and she produced the numbers.

It was also clear that we needed to accelerate our marketing efforts. Georgia had been in charge of Corporate Affairs at Chemical — which was appropriate since she had the most famous affair in the bank's history, with me — and had been in charge of the annual report. I will never forget her coming home and telling me that she'd had a meeting where people would not use a picture of Don Platten — a giant whom both Georgia and I loved while Chairman and CEO of Chemical Bank — because his teeth in the picture were yellow. She said, "His teeth *are* yellow!"

I took over marketing at Southern Financial and we started producing a quarterly newsletter, initially in black and white.

Georgia: *When Rod came on board he knew we had to sell our story. He thought it would be easy, but it wasn't at all. If we were to grow we had to buy other banks with our stock. So it was simple: we had to get investors to want to own our stock.*

Rod: When I joined Southern Financial in early 1998 I told the Board I really didn't need a large salary, but I wanted a very large stock option. They complied with both requests. Unfortunately the grant date on my option coincided almost exactly with the peak for bank stocks, and marked the beginning of the period when even grownup investors sold their real stocks and bought techs and telecoms. The period until the tech bubble broke in March 2000 was a painful one for us.

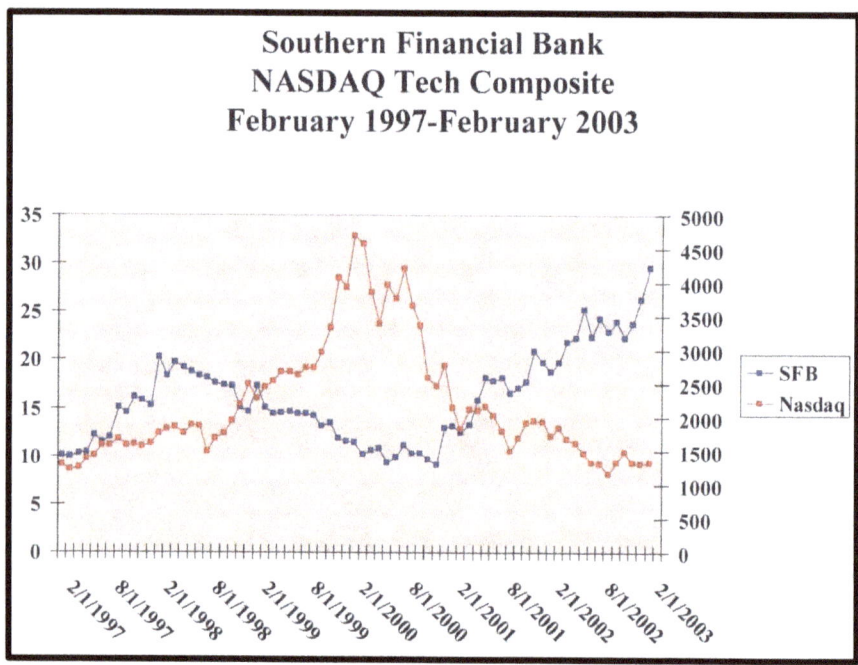

It was painful because we wanted to grow the value of our franchise through making acquisitions, after a 12-year slog through de novo branches, which are ones we open ourselves rather than buy. It's not possible to make cost-effective acquisitions unless your currency — your own stock price — is reasonably valued, plus there's liquidity in your stock.

In early 1998 Georgia and I set out to tell our story to the analyst community. We went to Richmond, Baltimore and Philadelphia and told our story to anyone who would listen. Remaking Iraq is a hard slog. Getting analysts to focus on your stock is even harder. We were in Philadelphia early on and made a great presentation and the analyst asked "Where's the sizzle?" We thought we had sizzle.

- We had a unique focus on small- and middle-market businesses.
- We were focused on the very best technology for our customer segment. For a small bank we were way ahead of the curve with web banking and creative uses of the internet.
- We were in one of the country's very best markets.
- We had a track record of flawless execution. We'd been profitable since our first full quarter of operation.

Not brain surgery or rocket science stuff, but solid. We learned that you had to say it over and over and we did. The other thing was that we actually believed it. Afterall, it *was* true — and it worked.

Georgia and I went up to New York at the beginning of my tenure to talk strategy with Sandler O'Neill. Sandler O'Neill was a firm that was founded just before Southern Financial by several partners who left Bear Stearns to go out on their own. I had known of them since the time I started at Greenwich Capital. It was one of two small investment banks that concentrated on financial institutions. The other was Keefe, Bruyette and Woods. My good friend Tom Kendall had introduced us to Steve Joseph on Sandler's fixed income side, even before I'd come on board full time with Southern Financial. Steve had been doing some trading with David deGive and we asked Steve to set up a meeting with Herman Sandler and other people on the corporate finance and equity analysis sides of the firm.

On that day we sat down in their conference room on the 104th floor of the World Trade Center in succession with Herman Sandler, Steve Joseph, Mark

Fitzgibbon and several other people from Sandler. We had sandwiches — this was before my no-carb diet — and salads. It was our first meeting with Herman Sandler, who was one of the most charismatic people we've ever met — and who bucked the trend of investment bankers not being terribly smart. Herman liked us and over the next couple of years would be a frequent source of wisdom, who kept us on the rails during what was to be a period of explosive growth for the Bank. Herman had an enormous zest for life, an incredible energy level and would erupt in a wonderful laugh from deep inside himself every couple of minutes. He adored Georgia and loved to tease me.

We were wrestling with the whole technology thing. We believed we were at the head of the pack in technology. We told them what we were doing in online banking and in our joint venture with the website hosting with Piedmont Press.

We knew an internet bank in common. Dave Smiloh had taken over a very sleepy Virginia S&L and made it into an internet bank when the internet craze was just beginning. He'd renamed it Telebank. His stock was soaring and ours was in the doldrums. Should we try to become an "internet bank" too?

Herman had a practical solution. He said we should just spend this year's earnings and a bit more on advertising and we'd also be an "internet bank." (**Georgia:** *I said there was no way we would lose money that we'd worked so hard to make. I told Rod to forget his "internet bank." In hindsight I was a genius.*) We — primarily Georgia — were disabused of the idea, put our noses back to the grindstone and returned to Virginia to do what we needed to do.

That said something important about Herman. Investment bankers don't get paid unless their clients do a transaction that results in a fee. It's uncanny, but most of the time when you talk strategy with them they advise you to do something. Here was Herman subtly telling us to go home and not do anything different from what we'd been doing. Sandler O'Neill paid for the sandwiches.

Georgia: *We knew we had to find other banks to buy, and Sandler O'Neill couldn't really help us there. The banks we could afford were so small they were under Sandler's radar.*

But before long Rod had a parade of regional investment bankers who would come into our office at 37 East Main in Warrenton to tell us which banks were or which could be available. If we liked them Rod and I took them to the Second Street Café down the block for super lunch for four that cost about $20. We looked at a bunch of opportunities. Some good, some distressed. Rod is the eternal optimist, thinking we'd find the pony under the pile of manure — and eventually we did, but I'll let Rod tell that story.

Rod: Before I came on board, with Georgia essentially running everything, it simply had not been an option to make any acquisitions. We ultimately made five, but none of them were easy. We worked on probably 10 or 15 others that did not happen for various reasons. In retrospect it is amazing that we pulled off five cost-effective acquisitions.

Our first attempt failed. It was the Security Bank in Manassas. It would have been a deal made in heaven. Eric Hovde, who owned through his funds big positions in both banks, introduced us. They had two branches in Manassas and at the time we had none. We had done more lending in Manassas than they had. They had some problem assets that we believed could have been fixed.

We reached a tentative agreement on price and the social issues with their Chairman and their CEO. We spent an entire weekend doing due diligence. They decided they needed a fairness opinion and retained Gary Penrose, who at the time was with Scott and Stringfellow.

Gary told them the price we were paying Security Bank's shareholders was too high. He told them that our stock would decline if we did the deal. He also told them that he could find another acquirer, presumably one who wouldn't pay too much.

He found another buyer. He sold Security Bank to F&M in Winchester several months later. F&M ultimately sold to BB&T. It would be intriguing to look back and see how big a disservice Gary did to Security's shareholders and to us. It cost us a year. I had words with Gary — not nice ones either. I told him that I had been an investment banker with Morgan Stanley and I knew how they were motivated, but that what he had done had gone beyond the pale. Shortly after this BB&T bought both Scott and Stringfellow and Craigie, an old bond house in Richmond. We were doing a ton of business through Martha McKee, an old Chemical Banker at Craigie, and Scott and Stringfellow was dying to get our business. We met some time later with John Sherman, who headed Scott and Stringfellow before BB&T took them over. He was a real gentleman we admired greatly, but we were frank in explaining our problem with Gary Penrose. We told him that we would continue to do business with them on the fixed income side and that we liked Cary Morris a lot. But we also said that it was going to be difficult to heal the wounds that Gary had opened. Gary cost Southern Financial a year. It was a serious setback. (Gary helped us on the Metro-County acquisition, but that was later.)

The Horizon Bank Acquisition

Some months after the Security Bank disappointment, we got a call from Bill McKinnon, of McKinnon and Company in Norfolk, who had been retained to sell Horizon Bank in Fairfax County.

Horizon Bank was to be our best acquisition. It was our first and it set us on the path to what Southern Financial ultimately became. We didn't have any idea what we were getting into when we did it. If we had known what the dynamics on the Board and the advisory board were we might have elected to pursue another course. That would have been a mistake. In this case ignorance was bliss.

When we came on the scene, Horizon Bank was a $140 million institution — more than half our size. Its problem was that Horizon had never made any money. They wanted to raise more capital to grow. They established a committee to determine what they were going to do. The committee was comprised of John Belotti; Rick Hall, their CEO who didn't want to do a deal; Bruce Jennings and Art Meyers. They contacted Bill McKinnon, who had an investment banking boutique in Norfolk, McKinnon & Co. The company is Bill, his son, a trader and an assistant. If there is anyone else I've done Bill an injustice. Bill has been doing investment banking in Virginia forever. He knows every CEO of every bank in Virginia and all of their important Directors. He knows where all the skeletons are and where all the bodies are buried, but like any discrete investment banker he won't always tell you.

Horizon retained Bill to advise them on what to do. He soon told them that they couldn't raise capital by selling their stock where they'd been trading it. He advised them that they would have to consider selling. He put together a book with all of the financial information on Horizon and sent it to all the potential buyers, including us. The ones who responded made presentations to the Committee in a conference room at Lansdowne, just outside Leesburg, Virginia. Georgia had a meeting with a customer and was deeply skeptical that we could ever do anything, given the Security experience with Gary Penrose. I went to the meeting alone and in retrospect it was a disaster. John Belotti said later (and I think I'm quoting him accurately), "I didn't have any idea what he was talking about, but whatever it was it wasn't banking." The big picture didn't work then or later with John. I respectfully submit I was talking about banking, but I had to learn to tone it down.

We got another bite at the apple about a week later and Georgia came. I guess she talked like a banker. I kept quiet. Later we took John Belotti and his wife Joan out to dinner at Frogs and Friends. We liked John and Joan a lot, and Joan really liked Georgia. That probably sealed the deal.

Unbeknownst to us there was a significant rift on the Horizon Bank Board. Art Meyers, Bruce Jennings and John Belotti were convinced the bank wasn't going anywhere and that they had to do something. Bruce told us he'd gone to three consecutive Board meetings with a typed resignation in his pocket. They had fired the CEO who preceded Rick Hall and the Board, in effect, was running the company. They had a powerful Advisory Board, which Rick Hall had cultivated and in turn, they were supportive of him. The Advisory Board was in conflict with the Board. One of the Advisory Board members, Tom Tracy, was the owner and CEO of a mid-Atlantic payroll company called PrimePay. PrimePay was Horizon's largest deposit customer by far. Tom Tracy was violently opposed to the merger with Southern Financial. He threatened to undertake a letter-writing campaign to the shareholders of Horizon, urging them to vote against the merger. Georgia and I had a very tense lunch with him and Rick Hall. But he didn't own a statistically significant amount of Horizon stock, and he ultimately backed down. In the end the Horizon shareholder vote took place and it was fine.

About two weeks before the closing we had the routine meeting with the Federal Reserve to go down the checklist of all of the things that had been done and what still needed to be done. It's generally a pretty boring meeting. But when we got to item #27, which was daylight overdrafts with the Fed, it attracted my attention. I said we didn't have any daylight overdrafts. Next.

Dave Goldman, who ran Horizon's operations, and who is still with Southern Financial today, stopped me and said that Horizon had very large daylight overdrafts because of PrimePay.

After the Fed meeting concluded I sat down with Dave and learned that Horizon had not one but two Fedwires, with the second being in PrimePay's office. When that information sank in, I grew more scared than at any other point in my life. PrimePay had the totally unfettered ability to transfer as much money as it wanted anywhere any day. It wasn't limited to the amount that Horizon had on deposit with the Fed because of Horizon's daylight overdraft line.

The next day Georgia, Bill Stevens and I went to Tom Tracy's office for what, up to that time, was the nastiest business meeting of my career. We told him that we were going to send one of Horizon's people to their office to approve all of their transmissions on the Fedwire. We also told him that we would provide him with software that would allow them to originate ACH payments to our wire department, and at that time we would remove their Fedwire. We were also going to put them on an analysis account to regularize their relationship with us. We told him that they were more than welcome to move all of their business to another bank.

He fulminated and he threatened. He said that we were going to destroy his business and that he was going to sue us. He said that we had acted in bad faith because we hadn't told Rick Hall that we were going to meet with him. We did everything we told him we were going to do. We never spoke again. He kept his company's accounts with us for over two years before taking them to another bank.

Georgia: With all that said, Horizon was probably our best acquisition. It was a good bank with very good people who we wanted to keep. Rick Steele interviewed everyone and we ultimately offered almost every one of their employees a job — often a different job and sometimes a bigger job.

Horizon had a telephone operator, Sally Husick, who was "the voice of Horizon Bank." Everyone knew her and her irrepressible personality. We didn't have any telephone operators; we had voicemail. So we put Sally in charge of credit documentation in the credit department in Vienna (Virginia not Austria). She was the best keeper of credit files that anyone ever had. Thank you, Sally. She was with us until the end and everyone loved her. At our parties Andre Fox played "Mustang Sally" and everyone, including Sally and Rod, would dance.

At the time, though, the Horizon merger seemed difficult. Horizon was a good bank and we kept all of its employees except their CEO, Rick Hall, who left shortly after the closing. Tom Grantham and Jackie Fitterer were with Horizon and became two strong pillars to Southern Financial's success, doing completely different jobs than they had done at Horizon and wearing multiple hats.

With Horizon we learned how to execute a merger. We stopped hiring for months before the closing to ensure that normal attrition would create openings, which could be filled by Horizon back-office people that would otherwise not have been needed. It worked superbly and all the Horizon people, with the exception of three, were still at Southern at the time of the Provident merger six years later. We also kept virtually all of Horizon's customers. With many of their customers we increased the scope of our relationship since we had a larger legal lending limit and a far broader product base. The Horizon acquisition changed Southern Financial and put it on the road to becoming a much stronger and larger institution.

TECHNOLOGY AND THE ACQUISITION OF DARIEN CONSULTING

(See Appendix E – "More Banking Technology for Our Customers")

Rod: The Spring of 1998, when I joined Southern Financial, was an interesting time. The second earth-shaking revolution in business during our careers was just beginning — the first being the revolution in the role of women, which Georgia won without even trying. This one was the use of technology to flatten the structure of entrepreneurial organizations and to vastly increase the productivity of managers in those organizations.

When Georgia and I joined Chemical Bank technology was limited to the telephone (which was pretty good), mechanical typewriters (which were not), mechanical adding machines (which were terrible) and white-out (which was a cure all). We also had telexes. I saw my first crude fax machine in Chemical Bank's Tokyo Branch in about 1971 and had no idea about how important it would ultimately become. It was a JiJi Fax, which was the equivalent of the AP newswire. However, since there were too many characters in Japanese for a ticker, they had to adapt the fax.

In 1998 the revolution in technology was in full swing. It changed forever how banking laborers handled paperwork. It also changed forever how low-level employees handled basic analysis. When Georgia and I were in the Chemical Bank Credit Department it was a laborious process to complete an analysis of a company's financial statements, even if it assumed that past trends would continue. The invention of Visicalc and its successors — Lotus, Symphony and Excel — revolutionized the potential for financial analysis, using multiple scenarios. However, it is still true to say "Garbage in, garbage out."

We believed that Southern Financial's competitive advantage was a fierce focus on medium and small businesses. We focused on doing everything a bank could do for those businesses. We wanted to ride the wave of the revolution in technology to move ahead of our competitors in this market segment. We believed, and ultimately proved, we could be nimbler and implement faster than the big banks. All we had to do was be smarter and more sophisticated than the big banks.

A couple of weeks after I joined Southern a pushy salesman for a company called Towne Finance named Dwayne Whitiak found his way into my office. They were pushing a receivables financing system that could be used on the web. It appealed to me. I saw the logic behind it.

Georgia: *I must admit that if Rod hadn't been at Southern I would never have let Dwayne in my office. I had no time for salespeople. With Rod listening to ideas we were able to expand our product array and ultimately the Bank itself.*

I had Georgia talk to Dwayne and we bought it. Georgia was tight as a tick — a Kentucky phrase for "cheap." But she sprung for this one. The upfront cost was minimal, around $15,000. Part of Dwayne's pitch was that he'd make calls with the loan officers to sell the idea to our customers. Georgia and the loan officers hated the idea, but it worked. Before very long we had a couple dozen customers using the system to finance their receivables. Unfortunately, it wasn't long before we realized that the software was archaic and neither satisfied our customers, nor provided us with the security we thought we had. Moreover, economically, it was a bonanza for Towne. The fee structure was patterned on factoring what was risky and very expensive so that factors collect fees out the wazoo. The low upfront cost was a come-on. Our customers weren't factoring material. This was just one of the types of financing we wanted to offer them. For most of them we probably already had first trusts on their business real estate — maybe equipment leases and an SBA loan. This was for us just one piece of the total relationship. We had utterly no interest in factoring, per se; we were relationship lenders. To the extent we could be secured we wanted to be, but ultimately it came down to the relationship with our borrower. We explained that to Dwayne. He brought his regional manager in for a meeting.

We wrestled with Towne Finance for months. There were elements in their idea that were promising, but their software design sucked. I wasn't getting anywhere.

I finally called Aidan Harland who'd been my first boss at Chemical Bank and who'd left there to start up the Darien Consulting Group, which evolved into a bank systems design company. (Aidan is a Brit who'd fallen in love with his first wife and Rowayton, Connecticut, right out of the University. He has lived in the US since then, but retains the accent of his father who was an Anglican minister.) Aidan was in Atlanta and Towne was not far away in one of the city's suburbs. I explained our dilemma and Aidan understood immediately.

A couple of weeks later I flew down to Atlanta and met with Aidan and then we went together to meet with Towne's senior management. It was at the height of the dot.com boom. We met all their senior people, many of whom were new hires. I tried to explain as carefully as I could that I felt that they had a great idea, but that their product sucked. There were three players when they got a customer: Towne, the lender (us) and the borrower. Towne was the only one of the three making any money — and was also somehow losing its corporate shirt at a rapid rate. Something wrong with this picture? It was the whole technology boom in Technicolor. They had the beginnings of a good idea. They had an IPO and were trying to prove themselves. They wouldn't listen to us talk about the problems in their system. Maybe they felt they just didn't have time. Sometime later they were bought by another company in the same business called Private Business for the cash they still had from the IPO. (We'll come back to Private Business.)

After the dysfunctional meeting with Towne I had dinner with Aidan. He and I had professionally gone our separate ways after he left Chemical, but we had always remained close friends and in touch. Darien Consulting had become a very successful software provider of international trade and payments systems for large banks. His clients were the second-tier large banks. Manufacturers Hanover, for example, was a client, but when they merged with our alma mater, Chemical Bank, they dropped Aidan's system and used Chemical's in-house system. At the time of our dinner he had 14 or 15 bank clients, down a lot from his peak. But as a practical matter the number of banks with International Departments in the US had dwindled a lot. There couldn't be many more than 100 or a 125 left. Aidan had a market share of over 10%, which was incredible.

During dinner, when we went from white wine to red, I told Aidan, "You're making buggy whips. They're the best buggy whips in the world, and you have a great market share, but there's no place to go." I told him that he should join us and develop software that had a potential market of 10,000 banks rather than a hundred and change.

He was willing to listen. He'd toyed with the idea of developing mortgage banking software. I told him that everyone was doing that, but no one was writing cash management software for small businesses. We talked and negotiated over the next couple of months. Georgia was easy. She said I could do whatever

I wanted in technology, but it can't cost Southern Financial any money. Easy? In the middle of the dot.com bubble? Multiples in the hundreds?

Eventually Aidan, Darien's co-owner Jacques Smith, and I negotiated a deal that proved to be excellent for us. (Jacques also lived in Atlanta. I'd met him years before. He was an exceptional person, and became absolutely critical to the future success of Southern. He and Aidan are the only techies I ever met who could also talk.) Southern Financial bought Darien Consulting for stock. Darien Consulting would continue to service its International Trade clients and seek new ones that would pay its freight so Georgia wouldn't kill me. But our key mission would be to develop in-house cash management products to be used by Southern Financial and its middle-market clients.

Both Aidan and Jacques moved to Warrenton and bought houses in the Warrenton ex-urbs. They got to work right away. I told them that their first job was to build something to replace the abortion of a system we were using from Towne Finance. They were never to see it lest they'd be corrupted and try to copy it. Equally importantly, if they never saw it we couldn't be sued for copying it. The system, which evolved from this modest beginning, was ARTS/WebLockBox — a collaboration between Georgia, me and our loan officers, with Aidan and Jacques. It was iterative. We'd have a good idea that affected everything we'd done and everything we'd plan to do. It was probably a nightmare for any well-schooled systems designer.

At its core were two brilliant but pragmatic ideas.

First, our customers using Towne were supposed to enter each of the receivables they wanted to factor into the Towne system on the web. They already had to enter them into their own accounting system. They hated doing it again, so they didn't. Because of Towne's fee system it also cost them money when they did. And they committed legal fraud to avoid it. Aidan and Jacques' blindingly brilliant idea was to have the customers upload all of their receivables data to our computer once or twice a month. It would take them minutes to do it all. Once we had their data from Quickbooks, MAS90, Deltec, Peachtree or any of a half-dozen other small business accounting systems, we knew everything they knew about their receivables — unless they were trying to defraud us. (We ultimately learned that the customers who said they couldn't upload were trying to game the system.)

The second brilliant idea solved the problem of lockboxes for middle-market customers, using technology in a very creative way. Lock boxes have been around for big companies since the beginning of Georgia's and my careers. Conceptually they're simple: the bank receives a check and a stub from the post office; the bank picks up the mail, opens it and sorts it by customer, then deposits the check in the customer's account and creates a tape to tell each customer how much they received from which customers.

It's easy to do with computers. What's hard is how to deal with the inevitable human imperfections: when the amount of the check doesn't match the stub, when there is no stub, when the payee on the check doesn't match the stub. The devil, and the labor expense, is in the details.

Aidan and Jacques' brilliant idea was to finesse the whole matching problem and let our customers continue to do it themselves. We would download an image of each check and stub received each day to a private secure website which could be accessed 24 hours a day by the customer. They could then update their accounting records whenever they wanted. They already have to update their accounting records when they open the envelopes with their receipts. The only difference is that they'd have to open the website to look at the checks and the stubs, instead of opening the envelopes.

ARTS/WebLockBox proved to be an enormous success. Our fees from the system paid for our development costs a couple of times over every year. I pushed Devon, Aidan and Jacques to move on and to make ARTS/WebLockBox the core of an in-house cash management system that would be the absolute best in the industry. We came close. As a bank we were an absolute peanut compared to any of our competitors. The difference was that we all believed we could do it.

One Deal We Didn't Do

Georgia: *Over the next several years we looked seriously at maybe a dozen deals we didn't ultimately do. We knew we needed deposits. We were always able to grow our loan portfolio because we'd grown into a serious small-business and middle-market lender. Our deposits were growing, but not as fast as our loans.*

The most interesting deal we didn't do was Virginia Savings Bank in Front Royal. Front Royal is a different country. It was the capital of the "Free State," which resulted from the Whiskey Rebellion in 1794. It is my contention that Front Royal has been a little weird since the Rebellion.

We were introduced to Virginia Savings Bank as early as 1997. They were controlled by an old Front Royal native by the name of Ronnie Gillam. I went out to Front Royal with Dave Campbell, who was our President at the time, and met with Ronnie. He controlled the Board of Directors and was periodically replacing the management. He lectured us on how a bank didn't really need to make loans. It was enough to buy US Treasuries. We concluded that further discussions would be a waste of time and we left. Dave Campbell kept in touch with VSB after he left us and a couple of years later the Office of Thrift Supervision brought him in after they did a supervisory agreement, not with the bank, but with Gillam. Dave was supposed to see if the bank could be brought back to health. He concluded fairly quickly that they couldn't and set up an auction handled by Ron Riggins, an investment banker based in the District of Columbia.

They called us and asked whether we'd like to have a look. We said we would and put together a due diligence team comprised of Rod and me, and Rick Steele and Bill Stevens, who had just joined us. We spent the next week in Front Royal reviewing their credit files, their lease commitments and their books — all things a bank typically reviews. The most entertaining documents were their Board minutes and, especially, their OTS exam reports. The OTS reports are confidential, but also the most compelling well-written documents I've ever seen penned by government officials. If they can be declassified they should be made into a Harvard Business School case.

Ironically it was the OTS that was the proximate cause of their failure. It's hard to remember it today, but in early 1999 the Federal Reserve and the OTS were utterly hysterical about the potential for systemic problems beginning on January 1, 2000. They drove us and all the other banks absolutely crazy.

They scared the bejesus out of Ronnie Gillam and his Board. They cancelled a perfectly adequate service bureau contract and bought new hardware for $1 million and new software for nearly as much. But they couldn't ever get it hooked up. They had to hire consultants and get a new service bureau to keep operating. At the time we did due diligence the computers and presumably the software were still in their shrink wrap. One of our key issues in making our bid was whether they were worth anything at all. It was a serious issue since, as I recall, the bank's capital was around $3 million.

We ultimately made a serious offer. But we weren't willing to give them our stock because we were concerned about the potential for years of litigation. We offered them cash instead. The Greater Atlantic Bank out of DC, a much smaller institution, bought them for stock. We haven't heard of any litigation so maybe they were right.

First Savings Bank of Virginia

Rod: Our second acquisition, First Savings Bank of Virginia, proved to be the diametric opposite of Horizon.

First Savings was a small S&L that had started about the same time we had. It had two branches, one in Springfield and one in Fredericksburg. It was controlled by Barbara and Mark Fried. Barbara was an attorney and was Chairman of the Board of First Savings, while Mark was — and is — a spectacularly successful commercial real estate developer. (Their son is a successful residential real estate developer in the Fredericksburg area as well.)

Georgia: *In 1999 we'd known the Frieds for probably 10 years. We had nearly merged with First Savings in 1990 during the commercial real estate crisis. The day before the board meeting that would approve the merger, Rod and I met with Tom Walsh, our Partner at Price Waterhouse, and discussed the pros and cons of* *the deal. We were nervous. Tom asked me if I was sure Southern Financial would survive the crisis if we didn't buy First Savings. I said I was and Rod agreed. But neither of us were confident we would if the deal went through.*

That night we sat at our dining room table at Marblehead and talked it through. Tom had asked the right question. 1990 was a scary time in the banking business. FIRREA had just been enacted and S&Ls were being closed by the regulators every week. If we bought them and it worked it would save us a couple of years and we'd be on our way. The alternative was too risky. The next morning we told the Board and nixed the deal.

Who knows what might have been, but I remain convinced it was the right decision.

Rod: We remained in touch with Barbara and Mark during the 1990's, but once the crisis abated and Mark had recapitalized First Savings, we could never get Mark near a realistic price — until 2000.

I think that Barbara got tired and in 2000 we reached a deal. We did due diligence and announced. After Horizon we were probably a little cocky because it seemed easy. There were a couple of alarm buzzers early on before we closed. We had agreed on a pay for stay fund, which is typical, to pay employees who wouldn't be kept on after the closing. I was on a cell phone standing on top of our sailboat, the first Georgia Bear, in Hopetown, when Barbara told me that the entire fund was being allocated to Jeff Constanz, the President and CEO of First Savings, along with two other senior employees. Jeff didn't believe that his contract payout was adequate. Barbara had been bamboozled and I was batshit — or "upset" for you non-boomers.

After the regulatory approvals, but just before First Savings' shareholder vote, Georgia, Bill Stevens and I spent a day at First Savings' Springfield headquarters to do a loan-by-loan review that would determine which loans were impaired and should be written down at closing. We sat in a small conference room adjacent to a small office suite used by the First Savings commercial lenders. Georgia and Bill sat on one side of the conference table with stacks of credit files and the "Loans to one borrower" list, which is a standard bank management report. I sat on the other side of the table with my PC and built a spreadsheet to tally up the charge-offs we would recommend.

We were familiar with most of the credits since we had reviewed them during due diligence. When we found a credit we were unfamiliar with or where we needed an update we would review them with Jeff Constantz or the loan officer.

We did due diligence in February. We came back in June just before we were ready to close to have a last look at the loan portfolio. Perhaps we were a little worried because we had seen a memo from Jeff to First Savings' Credit Committee, which mentioned certain credits that could be fixed through "the miracle of purchase accounting."

Georgia: Rod, Bill Stevens and I were sitting in First Savings' small conference room in Springfield with stacks of credit files. Rod's job was to maintain a spreadsheet to tally the amounts that we were going to tell their Board to reserve against. Bill and I would go through the credits to see whether there had been any deterioration since our initial due diligence or whether we needed any additional information. Rod would record the decisions on his spreadsheet.

We proceeded rapidly through the list, but found some unexpected problems. One name kept recurring in several variations. Rod lumped them together on his spreadsheet suspecting that they must be related. At one point he asked one of First Savings' senior lenders to talk to us about one of the entities. His narrative was disturbing. My response was that it sounded like a company in search of a business. The lender basically agreed. I asked why we hadn't ever heard this name before? It wasn't on the loans to one borrower list the last time we were there.

He said that up until recently it had been in an overdraft. When we asked the amount of the overdraft, they responded that it was $750,000. There were several other companies involved in this and the credit was never approved by the board. In fact they were never notified at all.

Rod: The lender left the conference room. Georgia, Bill Stevens and I caucused. How bad could this be? We had no way of knowing except there was a hole in the balance sheet of at least $750,000. We called Barbara Fried who was stunned. After she talked to Jeff and the Board and did her own digging she called back and agreed that they had a problem. It was incredibly awkward. Their shareholders had already voted in favor of the deal. The Fed had approved it and we were waiting for the State Corporation Commission of Virginia's approval, which was expected momentarily.

Georgia: *Our attorney told us not to tell anyone. He said if we told the regulators it could delay everything. We ignored him and never used his firm again for anything. Rod said that we needed to call the Fed now and that was the right decision. We called our PSA (Principal Supervisory Agent) at the Federal Reserve in Richmond and said we'd like to come down tomorrow and talk to them and the Virginia State Corporation Commission at the same time. We didn't invite our attorney.*

The next day Bill met us at the Richmond Fed. We told them exactly what we'd found. Barbara had already told the OTS. She had, or was about to, dismiss Jeff and the other senior managers of the Bank. It was a matter of some urgency that we start running the Bank, although we hadn't legally closed on the deal. They asked what we were going to do about the $750,000. We said that we couldn't change the deal price because their shareholders had already voted. The only thing we could think of to do was to have Mark Fried, who owned at least 40% of First Savings' stock, plug the hole, but he hadn't yet agreed. The Fed thought it would be OK if he did.

(See Appendix F – "Breaking Banking Barriers")

Rod: The next day we had several very animated discussions with Mark on various car phones and he agreed to make the Bank whole for the after-tax cost of the loss. He ultimately sued Jeff Constanz and won! He wouldn't admit it but it was the best money he ever spent. The Frieds made an absolute fortune when we sold.

Capital Strategy

Beginning in 1998 Georgia and I had been trying to tell our story to the Bank stock equity analysts until we were blue in the face. We got to know a lot of them and they're warm, sincere people trying to do their jobs. But until they put pencil to paper or finger to keyboard and write about you, it doesn't help. In the great scheme of things it's better for them to write bad things about you than say nothing at all.

Bill Ridgeway at Anderson Strudwick in Richmond — bless his heart! — was the first to "discover" us. Thank you Bill! (Though you and your clients made a ton of money owning our stock.) Pride of place goes to him, but gradually other analysts discovered us.

Cary Morris at Scott and Stringfellow started to cover us, possibly out of guilt for what Gary Penrose had done. I really don't care; I was just happy to have Cary on board. After the two of them took an interest a number of firms began to cover us: Robinson Humphrey, Trident, Ferris Baker Watts, etc. By the time we sold we had over two dozen participants on each of our quarterly conference calls.

In 1999 we were invited to attend the Sandler O'Neill conference in Palm Beach Gardens. We weren't invited to speak, but it was a great opportunity to network. It was an even greater opportunity to listen to larger banks and appropriate their best ideas, which we did shamelessly. We're forever indebted to Herman Sandler and the firm for the opportunity.

The next year we went again, but not as presenters. It was at the time of the disputed election and the hanging chads in Palm Beach. In the interest of candor George Bush is our boy. We supported him early. We got him nominated with the "Warrenton meeting" and we got him elected on November 11th with our phone calls to Brit Hume from Palm Beach in 2000. If you hate him blame us. Our editor will decide whether we should expand on the story.

In early December 2000 we were back in Palm Beach for the Sandler O'Neill conference. On December 8th we attended the conference in the morning. If you didn't want to play golf in the afternoon you were invited to go out with Herman Sandler on the *Diamond Lady*, a serious charter yacht chartered to replace Herman's, which was having an engine replaced. (The previous year Herman had taken a small group on his boat, the first *No Problem*.) We didn't want to play golf and accepted the invitation to go out on the yacht. Herman drove us there in his black BMW convertible. The only other guest was Dan Healey from NorthFork. It was a magical afternoon. Herman's captain took the *Diamond*

Lady up the ditch — the inland waterway — and back. We had lunch. We watched the cable news channels, drank some wine and talked about the election. Herman wasn't a committed Bush supporter like Georgia, Dan Healey and I were, but we worked on him. For us the most important result of the afternoon was that Herman convinced Georgia that sailboats were a stupid idea. He showed her that motor yachts have bath tubs rather than showers. He asked her how long it took us to get to Bimini. Herman said that he could get there for lunch and come back. Within six months we'd sold our classic old Hinckley sailing yacht and bought the motor yacht, which we still have.

In the early evening, after the outing on the *Diamond Lady*, Herman met Georgia and me at the Amici Restaurant in Palm Beach. We were considering the purchase of a small leasing company near Richmond, and we wanted to talk to Herman about it. We told Herman and he basically said we were nuts. We could never make the company into a serious contributor to our earnings. We talked about how much the company we wanted to buy fit our business model, and how much it would add in terms of business development. Herman kept saying we were crazy. After three hours we wore him down and he agreed. For those of you who know Amici it was a wonderful place to have a discussion, and they have a marvelous chicken cutlet Bolognese. I think Herman enjoyed every minute of it. I know we did.

Ten days later, we did due diligence on the leasing company. The fit was perfect, but the bank couldn't stand the cosmetics and we withdrew. Herman's gut had been right.

Racing in the Poconos

In September 2000 Jeff Smith was the Sandler O'Neill equity analyst who covered our stock invited us up to the Poconos International Speedway and attend Sandler's private NASCAR driving school for a day and a half. We decided to go. It wasn't like anything we'd ever done, or like anything we'd ever wanted to do, but it would be a new experience. And we liked Jeff immensely. He was a sailor, had spent a lot of time in Florida and was someone we could relate to. If anything, he was much too gentle to be a cutting-edge equity analyst.

There was no way he could ask the questions that Ken Puglisi, the Sandler O'Neill partner who was to cover us later, routinely did.

We got to the hotel the night before and repaired to the bar where we found Tom Sipple, an old Chemical banker and friend whom we hadn't seen for years. Tom was with a bank in New Jersey and who was also a guest. Tom, unlike us, was a car racing enthusiast. We had a marvelous time with Tom. Jeff also arrived early and we talked to him. The other guests gradually trickled in. Eventually we had dinner and they brought in the head of the program and several of the drivers. They made a presentation about what we were going to do and they talked about their concerns that the track would be wet in the morning. They also talked about how proud they were that they hadn't had any fatalities, ever.

The next morning we had a conference call where we were closing a difficult sale for the bank of some property — ironically the property included a go-cart track — to repay a problem loan. It seemed preferable to getting to the track in time to prepare for the racing school. We completed the sale and headed out to the track.

We were too late to go in the racing school where we would drive ourselves. They suited us up to go out with a pro for several circuits of the track. Before we went we had to sign various releases for the school and for Pocono Raceway. Basically they said if you get killed you're shit out of luck. Jeff walked by while we signed them and said ruefully that his wife would kill him if she knew he'd signed them, too. They had two children under 3.

I went first. It was terrifying. When I went into the turns I thought the centrifugal force would make my car roll over. The drivers were fantastic. They drove less than a foot off the concrete walls. I never want to do it again, but I will remember it forever, particularly in light of what happened to Jeff in the World Trade Center.

Georgia: *I went next after Rod got out of his car. His face was a total blank, which I didn't think was good. I did my laps and couldn't stand the stress. I said later to Rod that we have enough stress every day. Why do we want to do this? But some guys, including Jeff, loved it.*

Rod: By early Summer 2001 our stock was finally trading well. It had been whacked after the Horizon Bank acquisition when some of Horizon's big shareholders dumped our stock. Our ownership was just too narrow. Most of our old shareholders were happy as clams and never bought or sold. We needed more float in our stock, i.e. shareholders who would buy *and* sell so that we wouldn't be vulnerable in future acquisitions to shareholder selling. If we were going to continue to grow we needed more capital. We didn't have anything in the hopper, but we believed that we would. Moreover, we believed that another secondary offering could broaden and deepen the institutional ownership in our stock. I thought that we should do some kind of a convertible preferred deal to avoid, to the extent possible, diluting our existing shareholders, including us. In mid-June we had Steve Joseph and one of the Sandler O'Neill analysts down to talk about our options. They spent a couple of hours in our Boardroom with Georgia, me and Trish Ferrick, our CFO, looking at our alternatives using their model. We liked it enough that we agreed to go up to New York and meet again in early July.

THE SECONDARY OFFERING (2001)

Rod: Georgia and I flew up to New York on July 9th and spent the night at the Regency Hotel. We went down to the World Trade Center the next morning. The security there was incredible. You had to stand in line in the ground floor lobby, and you couldn't get in unless you had clearance from the person with whom you had an appointment to visit and you had a picture ID. If you had both of those things they made you a new WTC ID for the day. Georgia and I both have and carry the picture IDs we got that day. We're not sure why. We'd both been there dozens and dozens of times before.

These are our picture IDs, albeit somewhat faded:

We took the elevator up to the sky lobby on the 78th floor and then to Sandler O'Neill's office on the 104th floor. We met with Steve Joseph and some junior Sandler O'Neill analysts for a couple of hours, running different assumptions through the Sandler O'Neill model to reassure ourselves that it wasn't a stupid idea to raise additional capital. It was a very big step for us and there are ultimately no easy answers in business.

Herman Sandler joined the meeting just before lunch and took us all back down the elevators to the Plaza and then over to the World Trade Center Marina, where he was keeping the latest *No Problem* that summer. This one was bigger than the one we'd been on in Palm Beach. It was Italian made, and a "Leopard," which was a make we'd never seen before.

Everyone but Steve Joseph relaxed and put on *No Problem* shorts and t-shirts, and we sat on the aft deck and had sushi and a glass of wine. Nine years later I still have the *No Problem* shorts.

In short order we disposed of our remaining business issues. I said that I thought it would be a good idea to do a convertible preferred issue. Herman said it will mess up your balance sheet and cap the potential appreciation of your common. He was right. I capitulated and concentrated on enjoying a beautiful afternoon.

Georgia: *I adored Herman. He was incredibly charismatic and I think he enjoyed the afternoon as much or more than anyone else. He had the Captain take the boat down New York Harbor to the Statue of Liberty. He loved being with people he liked, he loved good conversation and he loved boats. At one point in the afternoon he said, "It doesn't get any better than this." And it doesn't.*

We still have our No Problem shorts and shirts. I even have some No Problem hats on our boat but they're from an earlier trip.

Rod: We left New York for Virginia to put in motion all of the things we needed to do to get the offering underway. Mostly we were to put everything in Trish Ferrick's lap. The Board had approved it and now she had to do all of the work.

Georgia: *We were to return to the World Trade Center Marina just a month later. My sister Diane was to marry Dennis Ryan on August 11th on a yacht. My family loves weddings and this one was over the top. The Yacht was to leave the World Trade Center Marina at 4:00 pm. Just before the departure there was a service with Judge Collabella, who had been a family friend for years. My father was still alive and this was to be his last family wedding. The yacht took the same route that No Problem had taken a month before down to the Statue of Liberty. But once there it circled and the DJ played patriotic songs including Ray Charles singing "America." It was incredibly corny, but enormously affecting.*

Afterward the Captain cruised up the East River and then finally back to the World Trade Center Marina. It was magical. Dennis and Diane simply couldn't have had a better wedding.

Rod: After the wedding we went back to Virginia to finish up the S-1, but more ominously to see if we could settle the Washington Bike matter. (The owner of Washington Bike ultimately won the case, but the verdict was dismissed by the judge.)

There was a lot of legal sparring, including a couple of all-hands meetings with the lawyers from both sides. Finally we got real. We dismissed the attorneys and sat in that bleak conference room with John Chang and his wife. He said he'd wanted to kill Georgia, to run her over with his car, but since then he'd become a member of his church. He said that he'd taken courses at George Mason and now understood why we couldn't have lent him any more money.

But he still wanted a lot of money to settle, and he wanted the bank to buy a piece of property he owned in Herndon.

Our last meeting ever with John Chang was in the conference room at our Georgetown branch on a Saturday in early September 2001. For whatever reason he didn't bring his wife. The branch was closed and the three of us finally cut a deal. He didn't get what he wanted and we didn't either, but that nightmare was behind us.

Our Trip to France

Rod: Two days later, September 6, 2001, we left for France and arrived at the Raphael Hotel on the Avenue Kleber. The Raphael is an old hotel that purportedly was an SS brothel during WWII. But the rooms are marvelous. We've stayed there for decades, and per usual we booked Room 208.

For the past several years I've kept diaries of our vacations so that we could remember where we went during each trip. This vacation, despite subsequent events, was no exception. The following recollections of those days, starting on the 6th, are excerpted from the diary:

We're to meet Fred and Susan Bollerer tomorrow for our barge cruise in the Loire valley. The next morning we take the TGV from the Gare Lyon to Macon. We then take a taxi to Branges.

Susan and Fred got to Branges a couple of hours before we did. It was a charming little town and together we checked out the boat and got ready to leave. The first night and the second day were absolutely magical. We went downriver on the Seille. We had tied up the first night at the Auberge de la Riviere where we had dinner. It was absolutely idyllic. The lush green lawn came all the way down to the river. The restaurant is a rustic old farmhouse and all of their food is raised or caught locally. The owner proudly showed us pictures of massive channel catfish he'd caught. We had poulet de bresse and cuisse de grenouilles. It was a great start to our shared journey.

The next morning Georgia and I jogged around the Auberge in the morning before we left. Heavy duty, serious, old-fashioned farms.

We took the boat downriver still wearing our jogging clothes. We've agreed that Fred will do the cranking in the locks and I'll drive the boat.

Just before lunch, we tied up in Cuisery and the four of us set out to provision the boat and to find a place for lunch. We bought marvelous bread, cornichons, pate, wine, lettuce and Dijon mustard. *And* we found a wonderful place for lunch, the Hostellerie Bressane. Fred and Susan looked fine, but Georgia and I were in our grubby jogging clothes. As it turned out, the season was over and they were ecstatic to have us. And a wonderful lunch it was.

After lunch we continued down the river to Torchere where we spent the night. It is a nice town with the locks that allow the transit from the Seille to the Saone. Dinner was OK. The next morning Georgia and I jogged to a wonderful flea market where we added some corkscrews to our collection and then across the river where we met some very serious French dairy cattle.

Later that morning we transited the locks, which took us down to the Saone and started our trip up the Saone. The next two days were cold and drizzly and I drove the boat from the upper deck with Fred, Georgia and Susan coming up periodically to keep me company.

Georgia: *We had a lot of fun laughing at Rod sitting on top of the boat in the rain. He refused to bring warm clothing on the trip and was freezing. Susan and I ran inside periodically and put on the heater. Rod finally gave in and said he* *needed to buy a sweater in the next town. The only problem was that the only store in the town was a general store and Rod bought the only sweater they had for $20.*

(See Appendix G – SFB Newsletter "On the Move")

September 11th

We tied up last night in Seurre. A very small town. Georgia and I jog around the town and return to the boat. We went on our way. The day starts badly with a near disaster in a very difficult lock. In the early afternoon we tied up in Auxone and had a walk around the town. I wanted to stay the night, but Fred, Susan and Georgia unanimously wanted to continue downriver and we did. There are absolutely no nice restaurants here.

So we leave Auxonne and proceed downriver to Lamarche sur Saone where there is supposed to be a very good restaurant with a small pontoon for two boats.

We get there just before 3:00. The dock could accommodate two boats. There was already a boat tied up belonging to an elderly British couple. They helped us with our lines. While Fred and I were getting us seriously tied up Georgia was standing on the cabin sole, which was as high as she could go, to get a signal trying to call Trish to see how the Sandler O'Neill offering was going.

"What do you mean it's not filed yet?" "My God!" We stood there with Fred and Susan for the next two hours while the events unfolded. The elderly British couple put on the BBC World Service on a scratchy radio and we stayed on the phone.

We heard from Trish what was happening from Bloomberg as it happened and we heard it on an old radio from the BBC World Service. The BBC sounded more horrifying than what we were hearing from Bloomberg. We heard everything as the towers collapsed.

We got Devon on the phone, safe in a very jittery Georgetown, with humvees on M Street. The Pentagon is about three miles from our Georgetown branch.

At about 10:30, New York time, I called Steve Joseph's home phone number and got Angelique. She hadn't heard from him and was totally distraught. We knew that Steve was habitually late and he was the only one of our friends we'd expected to find alive. After talking to Angelique we began to understand how awful this was to be for us.

We talked to Georgia's mother Rose and found that Georgia's brother George had managed to evacuate all of the people from his company in downtown Manhattan, next to the World Trade Center, and was on his way home. He'd seen the people jumping from the windows of the World Trade Center as he was evacuating his own people.

We even found my brother, Lance, on his cell phone. He was in New York on business and saw everything from the West Side Highway on his way downtown. It is a different world. We're 3,000 miles away on a barge in backward, rural France — he's in Manhattan, but we're networked almost instantly. Think about that.

We talked to Rick Steele and Dave Goldman several times to formulate contingency plans to assure the security of the Bank. We hired armed security guards for key branches.

When there was nothing left to do, the four of us walked a mile and a half into the little town down the road from the restaurant where we'd tied up. The town had a bar with a television and Georgia and I and Fred and Susan gratefully entered it. About a dozen locals were sitting in silence in the bar watching the single television and we joined them. We watched the images of people jumping from the towers, the planes hitting the towers, the towers collapsing, a large white yacht leaving the World Trade Center Marina and the chaos on the ground over and over. The locals were completely silent. We finally left to walk back to the restaurant.

***

Rod: At the Hostellerie St. Antoine the four of us ate a very somber dinner. Devon said much later that Georgia and I were too affected by what happened at the World Trade Center. Maybe that was true. But the two of us weren't affected as much by what happened at the Pentagon. My mother and father had both worked there during WWII, but I'd never been there except possibly in early utero. We didn't really know anyone who died there, but we knew more than a dozen who died — who were killed, including Herman Sandler and Jeff Smith — at the World Trade Center.

Georgia and I also had emotional ties to the World Trade Center. Jim Hillestad and the Creative Services Group that had reported to Georgia had been there. We'd eaten a half-dozen times in the Windows on the World restaurant with Alfonso Finocchiaro, and probably another dozen times with other people. Cantor Fitzgerald was there. I'd seen Bernie Cantor's sculpture collection. I'd dealt with them for years. I'd gone over there when I was with Chemical to evaluate Telerate, which started operations there in the early 1980s. It was a part of our lives. We all live in a conceptual space and the World Trade Center was part of ours.

More recently we'd visited the towers with Sandler O'Neill probably a dozen times. Now they were obliterated. Cinders. How do you deal with that?

That first night we were numb. We were just beginning to understand what a cataclysmic event it was for us. In the middle of dinner we got a telephone call I think from Trish or David, who told us Steve Joseph of Sandler O'Neill had survived. He'd taken the elevator down, changed at the 78th floor and made it. He told us about it later. It was a moment of joy and relief for us amid the worries for everyone else.

Before we left the restaurant, the chef/owner who was French/Algerian came out from the kitchen and told us how awful he felt, how much he supported Americans and his concern that this was a serious problem with the Muslim world. It was quite a prophetic statement.

Georgia: *That night we knew we wanted to get back to Paris as soon as possible. We would have real phones and email. We could connect to the people back home.*

Rod: The next morning we untied the boat and headed back to Gray in an attempt to get back to Paris as soon as we could. We covered what would have normally been a two-day leg in one. We tied up in Gray that night, had dinner and slept fitfully.

The next morning we took a taxi to Dijon where we bought all the papers. We then took the train back to Paris. On the way we talked on a cell phone to Steve Joseph of Sandler O'Neill, a reporter from the *American Banker*, our stockbroker, and our real estate agent concerning our upcoming sale of our Georgetown house and the purchase of a new one. It wasn't a relaxing trip.

When we arrived in Paris, Georgia and I returned to the Raphael and Fred and Susan to their hotel.

I called Dan Szor of FX Concepts France, whom I used to manage, and asked him whether Georgia and I could come over and use phones and email at their office for several days. Dan graciously offered us whatever we needed.

Georgia: *On Sunday the 16th Rod and I ran up to Montmartre. It was deserted. No tourists at all. We ran along the Rue des Abesses. We were the only people we saw. The church bells played Amazing Grace, then our National Anthem and God Bless America. We ran and sang along with the bells and cried.*

Rod: Left to their own, without the horrendous problems with their Muslim minority, the French are wonderful. With the scimitar of those problems they are awful, but they don't have any alternative.

For the next five days we went in to the FX Concepts office just 200 yards from our hotel at 46 Avenue Marceau. It was comforting. I'd spent a lot of time there in previous years. We went in every afternoon, and because of the time difference were able to talk to our office and Sandler O'Neill from late morning until the afternoon. Our initial objective was to save the secondary offering. Jim O'Meara of Sandler O'Neill had been at the printers on the morning of the 11th for a final proofreading of our S-4, which saved his life. The S-4 was filed with the SEC on September 12th. *Fortune* magazine published a magnificent piece on Sandler O'Neill, titled "Starting Over," in their January 21, 2002 issue. They mentioned a "long-planned secondary offering" filed on the 12th. That was us.

From the time we talked to Trish on September 11th we had serious concerns that Sandler O'Neill could do it. Many of their critical employees were dead. We'd been dealing with Robinson Humphrey, a firm in Atlanta, and we thought that it would be ideal to do a joint deal between the two. We proposed that to Steve and he responded in about 15 minutes saying that if we did that it would kill Sandler O'Neill as a firm and he begged (maybe too strong a term) that we continue with the firm as sole manager. It was probably the most difficult decision we ever made.

We had to consider our shareholders — including ourselves — as well as our employees and Sandler O'Neill. Our country had been attacked by terrorists. Sandler O'Neill had been attacked, too. But could we afford the risk of a failed offering?

We couldn't. However, for Herman Sandler; for Jeff Smith, who was our equity analyst and we'd gotten to know and like at NASCAR school in the Poconos; for Christy Irvine, who traded our stock; and for Steve Joseph, who was still alive, what should we do?

Sandler O'Neill's Investment Banker assigned to our deal, Tom Killian, was an uptight control freak, and we don't control easy. Their in-house attorney, Patty Murphy, who was assigned to the deal, was hostile and unhelpful. This may be insensitive, but Patty Murphy was borderline hysterical. Both Patty and Tom had had a lot of their friends die on September 11th — just as we had.

On the second or third day we called Tom Killian from the FX Concepts office in Paris and told him the deal was going to fail unless he could control his attitude, vis-à-vis the other investment bankers, and control Patty Murphy. We were not happy campers. We finally got a flight out of Paris on September 20th.

And with an enormous amount of trepidation, we decided to go forward with Sandler O'Neill as sole manager. Ultimately, the only reason we did was because we knew we had Jimmy Dunne's personal commitment that the deal would be successful. We knew Jimmy — though not as well as we knew Herman — and he is an Irish mensch. He was the only member of the triumvirate that ran Sandler O'Neill: Herman Sandler, Chris Quackenbush, and Jimmy Dunne, the only one of the three who survived September 11th. (He was playing golf with customers.)

We had met Jimmy several times. He was an old bond guy and we had a lot of common acquaintances. He is not subtle and nuanced, but he is a "real" guy and we clicked. Before September 11th he was in charge of risk for Sandler O'Neill and was their on-call asshole. He was the guy who made their tough decisions and made sure they survived. (You should read the *Fortune* magazine article about the firm, post-9/11. There's a lot of Jimmy in it and it's magnificent.)

Our deal was as critical to Sandler O'Neill's prosperity as it was to ours. The SEC decided not to review our S-4. That put us on track to do a road show in early October. To complicate matters we had sold our existing house in Georgetown and bought another. We closed on both on October 1st and moved the same day!

In the best of times a road show is like astronaut training. You see what the human body can absorb and how much stress you can withstand. When you are doing it less than a month after September 11, 2001 with Sandler O'Neill, it's far more challenging. We went to Milwaukee, Chicago, Pennsylvania, Baltimore, New York, Boston and Washington DC. We talked to any investor who wanted to see us and to some who didn't. There was an enormous amount of support for Sandler O'Neill. We saw a number of investors who wouldn't normally have seen a bank as small as we were. On the other hand many of our minders, the Sandler O'Neill salespeople who joined us in the meetings, and who would normally have briefed us on how to frame our story for each investor, didn't have a clue because the salesperson who covered that investor was dead. By the end we hated hearing each other talk. I faked Georgia out at one meeting by doing her spiel and making her do mine.

We finally finished our tour late in October while in Boston. Steve Joseph had been our minder that day. That was perfect. He is one of our very closest friends and there is absolutely no one we'd rather spend time with. After our last investor presentation we decided to go out for a drink before he flew back to New York.

Steve rejected out of hand my suggestion that we go to a bar that was on top of one of the big office buildings. We ended up instead in a nice bar in the basement of another building. Steve was one of 17 Sandler O'Neill employees who got out of the World Trade Center alive on September 11th. Sixty-six died that horrific morning. (Herman's body was found about a week later. He didn't ride down with the building.)

The Passing Game

Steve was a Vietnam War veteran. He'd almost died at least once in Vietnam. He told us he'd learned to trust his instincts. He had been in Sandler O'Neill's office on the 104th floor in 1993 when the bomb went off in the basement, the first time Al Qaeda had attempted to destroy the World Trade Center. Sandler O'Neill had only been in its new offices for a couple of weeks back then. Steve had evacuated like everyone else by walking down the stairs.

On September 11, 2001, the first plane hit Tower One at about 8:30 am. When he saw the smoke from the first explosion in Tower One Steve's first thought was that the smoke was coming toward Tower Two, where Sandler O'Neill was, and it would be in the building's air intake valves in no time. Herman Sandler said that anyone who wanted to leave should, but that he was staying. Steve's Vietnam-honed instincts took over. He briefly considered bringing his computer, but thought better of it, and just left. He took the elevator down to the sky lobby on the 78th floor just before 9:00 am, and then took another elevator down to the ground floor. The second plane hit Tower Two at 9:03 am, near the 60th floor, minutes after Steve descended. The quick action saved Steve's life.

He walked home. He couldn't get through to Angelique on his cell phone so she didn't know whether he was alive or dead until he rang the front door bell in their apartment. In the interim, we'd called Angelique from France and she was anguished and distraught.

We finished the evening with Steve emotionally exhausted and walked back to our hotel.

The next morning, we woke up to return to Washington. Georgia bathed and I packed. Then it was my turn to shower. As I finished up the hotel alarm sounded. Georgia was drying her hair. We opened the door and the hallway had people organizing the exodus from the building. Then the speakers began to say over and over "Evacuate the building! Evacuate the building!" Georgia remembered Steve's wisdom from the night before, scooped her jewelry off the counter onto her purse, put her raincoat over whatever she had on, left her husband and joined the evacuation. It was 15 minutes before I got enough clothes on and joined her on the street. It was a false alarm, but we found what Georgia's priorities were.

(See Appendix H – Our letter to Jimmy Dunne at Sandler O'Neill. Jimmy sent it back with a warm note that read: "Found this yesterday after going over some correspondence from 9/11. Thank you again for using us and taking the time to write this.")

The offering was priced about a week later at $22.50. We were upset, thinking it was 50 cents to a dollar too low, and had a conference call with Jimmy Dunne. He had a clear opinion as did we and we ultimately decided to proceed. In retrospect it was one of the best things we ever did. We raised our goal amount including the "green shoe." It broke us out of the pack and put us in a different league.

Here's what happened to our stock price after the offering:

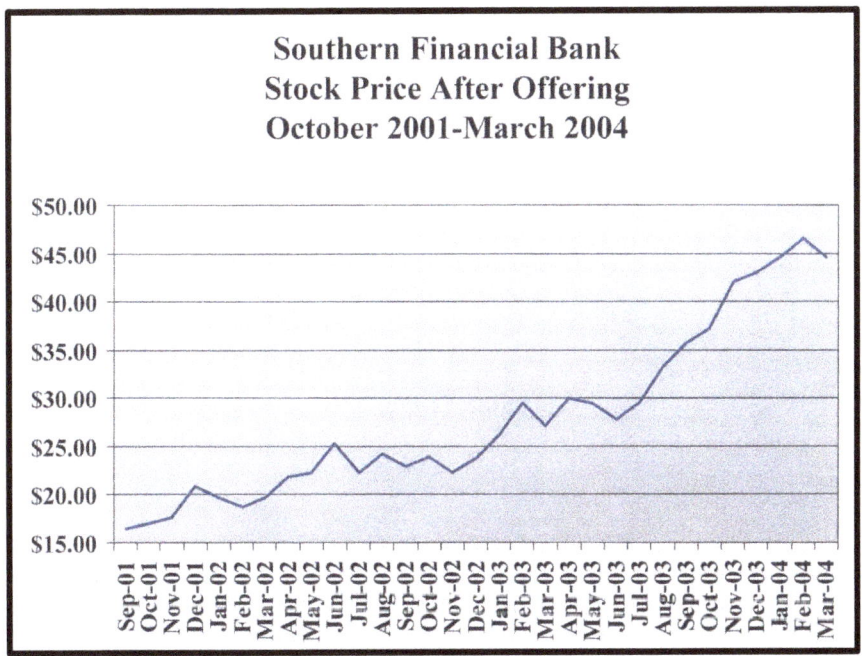

We had Christmas in Harrison, New York, with Georgia's family. Georgia's father was terminally ill and it was a painful holiday.

A week to 10 days later we got back to the farm. On the farm we have two fenced kennels in a several-acre enclosure, with a 7- or 8-foot chain link fence and a foot of barbed wire on top. We have Bichon Frise dogs and never needed anything like that. The previous owner had mastiffs and needed the fence to keep the dogs in. We owned Bichons Frises since just after we married. Georgia's poodle had died and we saw a Bichon Frise on the shore when we were off on our boat. That was enough to convince us to get one of our own.

Our first Bichon Frise was a female named Tia whom (I should probably say "which," not "whom," but she was a person — a little neurotic, but a person) we bought in Connecticut. Later we sold our place in Cos Cob and she moved with Georgia to Marblehead Farm in Virginia. When we decided to breed her we realized we couldn't send her off to any stud. So we bought, again in Connecticut, the male who was arguably the best Bichon Frise in the country. He had earned his championship at 18 months of age. His name was Ch. Huggy Bear de Tenerife. Bear entered our lives and became a part of them for the next 12 years before he passed. He lived up to his name. He was always affectionate, but he also had presence and dignity. He was always in control.

A lot of his descendants have his head and his carriage, but are utterly silly. Many of them have Tia's ditziness.

By Christmas 2001 we had six Bichons Frises. Bear and Tia were long dead, but we had their brood, and many of their descendants are scattered around Northern Virginia. Pee Wee Bear was a 10-year-old male who was getting decrepit. Zoo Zoo Bear was the matriarch by virtue of being the oldest female. Hato Bear was Zoo Zoo's daughter and was just under breeding age. We also had two of her litter mates, one of which was pregnant. Additionally we had R2D2, a male Bichon we'd bought to outcross with the Bear line. And we also had and still have a wonderful, but totally useless, English Springer Spaniel, G2. (Julia Woodson and Frank Woodson manage our farm. Julia and her family still call G2 "Georgia," which allows her to periodically say to me, "Mr. Porter, Georgia is in heat, can I lock her in the barn?" To which I invariably respond, "By all means, please do!")

We returned to Marblehead after Christmas in 2001. Three of the Bichons Frises were missing. Frank found them the next morning and called us. Hato and one of her daughters had been decapitated and left in their pen. One of their heads was gone, the other was attached, but just barely. Hato's pregnant daughter was gone entirely. I saw their bodies just before Frank buried them. Pitiful, agonizing and horrifying.

We can't see any of our neighbors' houses from ours on the farm. Nights on the farm are totally dark and quiet, completely the opposite of our house in Georgetown. We'd lived there since 1986 and nothing like this had ever happened.

The murder of our dogs shattered our feeling of being cloistered and protected even more than 9/11 had. The Bichons Frises were our friends who had entrusted their lives to us for three generations. If you know any Bichons Frises you know how they share your joy. You also know how they are their own people.

We called a couple of security services to investigate and they were useless and expensive. Finally we called Milton Harding, who was the husband of Joyce Harding, a long-time Southern Financial employee. Milton was a local magistrate who was just starting a private security service. With a couple of off-duty Fauquier County policemen — officers Grant and Cunho — Milton helped us stabilize our lives.

But it got worse before it got better. The day after we found the dogs Georgia started getting hang up calls in her office. They were coming in through the main number and asking for Georgia. Milton installed new equipment and established procedures for the tellers and we were able to record several of the callers, but the calls tapered off and stopped.

Even scarier was the fact that on at least one night we were followed home after dinner. At that time on Monday nights we ate at the Tadpole Café, Tuesdays at the Rail Stop in the Plains, and on Wednesdays at Frogs and Friends. It was a predictable pattern. One Tuesday we parked in front of the Rail Stop in the Plains. The Plains has maybe 75 inhabitants and the one nice restaurant, which Robert Duvall used to own, and one gas station/convenience store that is 50 yards from the restaurant. It's not the heart of a metropolis and we'd been going there since 1987.

A white pickup truck was parked on the street just behind where we always parked. A tall, thin Black man was standing next to it. We'd never seen him before. We went into the Rail Stop and had dinner. An hour and a half later we came out and the white pickup truck was still there and the man was sitting in the driver's seat. I walked back to get a look at him and he was the same man. I probably should have called the police and stayed there until someone came.

But I left and he followed us down Route 55 to the turn, and down the back road we always take home. We lost him on the twisting back road that we'd driven hundreds of times and which is red meat for a Range Rover. We called Milton on his cell and got Officer Grant there for the night. In the nights to come the off-duty officers spent a lot of time at the farm, and I made my nightly walks carrying my shotgun. We built a security gate that we probably should have put up a lot earlier. We also began to spend more time in Georgetown.

Georgia: *We never learned who was behind everything. For the first time I began to think that being well-known had its drawbacks.*

The Acquisition of Metro-County Bank

Georgia: *The Metro-County Bank was a $90 million bank with five branches in the Richmond area. Its Chairman and CEO was a 70- or 71-year-old (depending on which year of birth he gives), lifelong Richmond banker by the name of Stafford White. He was the son of a Baptist minister who had worked at First Virginia Bank and the Hanover Bank before founding Metro-County Bank in 1996.*

The acquisition was a delicate process. Just before our final presentation to the Metro-County Board, Gary Penrose, who acted as Metro-County's investment banker, said that we had to be more "genteel." We were perceived as being "gunslingers from the north," albeit the north of Virginia. That meant that I made the presentation and Rod didn't talk. No matter. We did the deal.

After that we always saw our Richmond clients in a different light. We believed that the community and family ties, which existed in Richmond much more than they did in Northern Virginia, would serve to restrain some peoples' inclination toward dishonesty. But it was not to be.

Rod: Several weeks after the closing we had lunch with Bob Davis, a customer of Metro-County's, at Byram's restaurant, across the street from our West Broad Street office. Stafford set it up and was there with Joe Kellum, and Oliver Lawrence, who was seeking to assume some of Bob's loans on the East Grace Street properties.

Oliver had already received some loans from us. We were a little worried about Bob and liked the idea of Oliver assuming the loans. He seemed to be a solid, successful, first-class guy — a former football player at LSU, local entrepreneur, longtime regional manager for Mobil, his wife an heiress in the Caribbean. We said we'd look at it.

Georgia: In this business we've seen the best and we've seen the worst. Some of our customers are absolutely wonderful entrepreneurs. They are brilliant, they grow their businesses, they're prudent and they're honest and they get rich. They are our heroes and many of them are our friends.

There are two other types. The first type fails gradually in business and begins to slide. This type can't tell us and just falls further and further behind. Eventually, we find out. Sometimes we pull them back from the brink and sometimes we don't.

They second type is every banker's horror story. They find a soft spot and set out to defraud the bank. They are the terrorists of our financial system.

Rod: Shortly after our lunch with Bob and Oliver a small Metro-County borrower by the name of Michael Crowder simply stopped making the payments on his three loans. It wasn't a big deal, until we realized he'd bought all the properties from Bob. The loans totaled $253,000 and we'd written off $100,000 just before we closed on the Metro-County Bank acquisition because one of the five properties had burned down and we weren't sure we'd be paid in full. Our exposure was peanuts compared to our $600,000,000 loan portfolio.

What was weird was that Michael stopped making the payments on *all three* loans at the same time and that he never declared bankruptcy. The deadbeats *always* go bankrupt, and it takes us an additional six months or even a year or more to foreclose, while they milk the properties for everything they can. But Michael Crowder didn't go bankrupt.

So we foreclosed in January 2002. We were in Richmond for a couple of days and Jackie Fitterer, who is a superstar who ran our Loan Servicing and Administration, called Georgia to tell her we owned the properties. She also told Georgia that we had a broker do drive-by appraisals on the properties and that his rough appraisal was much lower than the amount of our loans. He also told her that Michael had been ripped off. He'd paid far too much for the properties.

That morning we had two customer meetings with Joe Kellum, who we had hired to head up our commercial lending function in Richmond after the acquisition. On the way back to our West Broad Street office we called Stafford White and asked whether he'd like to join us for a casual lunch at the billiard hall just down the block from the branch. He said that he would, but why not Byram's, which was across the street from the branch. We said the food is better in the billiard hall. He laughed.

Stafford got there at about the same time we did, joking to Georgia that it was the first time anyone had worn a mink to lunch in the billiard hall. He was in high spirits. We kicked around various pending deals. Toward the end of lunch Georgia mentioned to Stafford that we'd just foreclosed on the Crowder properties and that our appraiser said Michael had been ripped off. Stafford asked who the appraiser was. Georgia called Jackie on her cell and told Stafford the name. It had been a referral from Metro-County. Stafford got agitated and said, "He's from Mechanicsville. He doesn't know shit from shineola about Richmond real estate."

Stafford then told us that Michael had bought some of the properties from Bob Davis. Over lunch a couple weeks prior Bob told us we "would be fine" on the Crowder properties.

I asked Stafford why Michael would have paid so much more for the properties than they were worth. Stafford said, "Maybe because he's Black and needed the credit." We had no idea at the time what he meant, but maybe we do now.

At that point I said, "We've got the addresses, lets go look at the properties." Joe Kellum agreed to drive and said he'd stop at the office to get a map. Stafford said that he knew where they were, that they were in Church Hill. We piled into Joe's car and went there.

Church Hill is a slum, but it's a gentrifying slum. Some of the nice old houses have been restored and they're working on some of the others. In a decade it may look like Brooklyn Heights from 30 years ago. But the Crawford properties weren't in Church Hill.

We asked a pedestrian where one of the addresses was and he said you've got to back across the river. They're off Hull Street. At that point Stafford seemed to tense up. He said he had a meeting at the Atlee office at 2:00 pm. It was about 1:15 and it was the first time he had mentioned the meeting. He demanded we drive him back to West Broad and we said no, that we would drop him off and he could get a cab back. He said he would come with us and made a big deal about calling the office to put off the meeting until 4:00 pm. It was at that point I whispered to Georgia that this whole thing was a scam.

We looked at four of the five properties and the appraiser was right. We drove back to West Broad in silence. We got back at 2:05 pm. If Stafford actually had a meeting he was all of 15 minutes late. He drove back to Atlee.

Back at West Broad we sat down with Joe and conferenced in Jackie to try to figure out what was going on. We realized that absolutely no one had actually ever seen Michael Crowder. Was he real? The file said his application had been taken by phone. He was a nurse who made $10.50 an hour. The application said he had $100 in cash to close. He needed immensely more than that if he was actually paying the price on the contract. We suspected he was a straw man for Bob.

I went out into the branch and asked the branch manager, Sylvia Loving, if she had ever seen Michael Crowder. She said she thought she had. He was Black and brought into her branch a form for her to sign so that he could collect the insurance on one of the five units, which had burned. (Arson?) She properly declined and sent the form to Jackie. Then she asked whether I knew that Michael was affiliated with Bob. I said that vaguely I did. She said that at her previous job at another bank she'd been told to watch everything Bob did since he had just gotten out of jail.

I went back into Joe's office where Georgia and Joe were still talking and called Milton Harding, whom we'd put on retainer after the dogs were killed. Milton called back shortly to say that Bob had served time at Fort Leavenworth in the early 1980s for bank fraud and arson. All of the information was in the public domain. We asked Milton to start digging. We also asked Jackie to reconstruct what had happened on the Crowder and Davis loans and left to drive back to Georgetown for what we hoped would be a relaxing weekend.

Our anniversary is February 6th and we'd planned to spend it in Annapolis to have a change in venue. But by that Thursday they were forecasting snow in Annapolis and we decided to spend the weekend in Richmond. We got reservations at the Jefferson from Friday through Sunday. We drove down and on Friday night we had dinner at TJ's in the hotel. On Saturday morning we set out for our morning run. The plan was to check out several of the Grace Street properties that Bob Davis owned and then explore Shockoe Bottom. We found the Grace Street properties and were appalled. One Grace Street property was supposed to have an operating restaurant in it. The restaurant was closed. Another Grace Street property was supposed to have been renovated. Nothing had been done at least from the outside. The whole block appeared to be derelict and vacant except for the leasing office. It was immensely worse than we could have imagined.

We spent the rest of the morning exploring Shockoe Bottom and the adjoining area and had lunch in an Irish pub in the Bottom.

After lunch we called Rick Steele, Jackie and Milton and asked them if they could come down for a meeting with Stafford Monday morning. All of them could. Jackie said she had completed a detailed spreadsheet covering who sold what to whom. We told them we would look at the other properties Sunday morning.

Saturday night we had a wonderful dinner at the Rivah Bistro talking about Stafford and Bob Davis — not exactly the things you should worry about on your anniversary.

The next morning we plotted out all of the addresses on Grace Street and Broad Street that we knew Metro-County had financed. We ran east on Grace Street and then doubled back on Broad. Our notes were as follows:

211, 213, 215, 217, 219 E. Grace Street
Sausalito Restaurant closed and for rent. All other retail derelict. 219 used as "Rental Office." Possibly some work in 219. It is occupied. Two upstairs windows replaced. No apparent occupancy of other upstairs apartments.

209 E. Broad
Retail space occupied by "2nd Street Market and Discount" — happiness! No apparent occupancy of upstairs.

103 E. Broad
"Living World Stage Co." occupies lower floor. Can't see what occupies upper floors. Is Davis here?

402 E. Grace
Downstairs occupied by "Uniform City." Upstairs derelict.

404 E. Grace
Beautiful old building but retail and everything else is vacant and has been for a long time. Next to Alan Furs' original location.

2 West Broad
Building razed. Vacant lot.

323 West Broad
Totally vacant. Oliver Lawrence construction notice on the front door. Some interior framing done.

Depressed by what we had found we ran down to Cary Street and had lunch at Mom's Siam, which has the best authentic Thai food *anywhere* except maybe

Chiangmai. We tried to get their account for the Bank, but couldn't convince them.

Georgia called Stafford on Sunday afternoon and asked him to meet us at the Jefferson on Monday morning at about 10:00 am. We told him we needed to understand what was going on with Michael Crowder and Bob Davis. He said fine, more calm than we were.

On Monday morning, Rick and Jackie got to the Jefferson about 8:00 am. Milton was there shortly thereafter.

Jackie then briefed us on what she'd turned up since we had talked to her last. She'd focused on Michael Crowder, Bob Davis, Oliver Lawrence, and a couple others we'll just refer to as Young and Reynolds. Bob Davis was using Young and Reynolds as a front for an unethical businessman. Jackie's spreadsheet with subsequent discoveries showed an extraordinary story of a daisy chain of self-dealing, with Metro-County either as a willing participant or as a dupe. It was a scam, but the bank had to participate for it to work.

Stafford arrived at about 9:45 am as cool as a cucumber and sat down with the two of us and Jackie and Rick Steele in the elegant Washington Board Room of the Jefferson Hotel. After we finished up, Stafford reiterated that he would do whatever he could do to help. He said he would contact Bob Davis and urge him to refinance his loans elsewhere. He didn't think that would be a problem.

Stafford left and we caucused with Rick and Jackie.

Milton left to check the files at the *Richmond Times Dispatch*. We had lunch with one of our Richmond Advisory Board members and drove back to Warrenton.

We were never able to figure out why Stafford would have made these loans. Our attention was soon focused elsewhere. We had other customer deals, the Annual Report, the 10-Q and the prospectus. We were negotiating to buy another bank. We had a Federal Reserve exam. We introduced Southern Cash Manager and started a brand-new International Department to be located in Richmond. All of us — Jackie, Rick, Joe Kellum, Milton and the two of us simply had too much to do to continue to worry about a possible problem, no matter how fascinating it might prove to be. But events kept carrying us forward.

Over the next couple of weeks Rick or Rod would periodically call Stafford and ask how Bob Davis was doing in refinancing the loans. Stafford would say that Tracy Jackson, who had been with Metro-County and then had left Southern Financial in a high dudgeon, was working on moving the loans over to Commonwealth Bank, which had just been acquired by Virginia Community Bank. Several times she told us that Causey Davis, the old President of Commonwealth Bank, would be there the next day to look at the Grace Street properties and that he wouldn't need an appraisal. On March 15th Rod called Stafford for one of our periodic updates. Stafford said that Commonwealth wouldn't make the loan because Bob Davis's wife wouldn't sign on the loan. Georgia reminded me that Davis is divorced!

Bob Davis was never able to refinance anything but he didn't default up through the closing on the sale of Southern Financial to Provident. After that we simply don't know. But two of the people he'd sold houses to at inflated prices did, and the losses taken by the Bank, in percentage terms, were staggering.

Like Michael Crowder, another First Savings client we'll call Johnson had also bought his properties from Davis or a Davis affiliate. Also like Crowder, Johnson didn't go bankrupt. We talked about it before the foreclosure. From the standpoint of the Bank we didn't really want to own the properties. But we thought they might be interesting investments for us personally with a lot of sweat equity. We talked to our son Devon and his friend Marc Harding, who lived in Richmond. They agreed and we set up GRDM LLC. "GRDM" stands for "Georgia, Rod, Devon and Marc." Georgia and I would lend GRDM the money if they bought anything.

Georgia: *The properties in question went to foreclosure before the definitive agreement with Provident. When they went to auction we instructed the Bank's attorney to bid amounts which would make us whole. He did, but in the open auction GRDM bid more and bought all of the properties.*

The Reynolds properties went to foreclosure after *the definitive agreement. We put it in Provident's hands. They would decide what the Bank was to bid on each property. Jackie Fitterer asked Mark Harding to get drive-by appraisals on each property, which he did. Provident's work-out department determined the amounts that the Bank's attorney would bid. Devon told us how much the maximum was that he would recommend that GRDM would bid on each property, without ever knowing what the Bank would bid. At the auction, another bidder won the two four family units and GRDM bought the rest.*

STRATEGY

Rod: In the great scheme of things our focus on small- and medium-sized businesses worked beautifully. We were able to grow our assets at over a compound annual rate of 20% per annum and our earnings at a comparable rate. Our flaw was that we could only grow our deposits at a 10% annual rate. Over time that creates a shortfall in your funding. You can cope with it for a while, which we did through very creative funding strategies, but eventually you have to do something to address the issue. Enter Essex Bancorp.

ESSEX BANCORP.

Our last acquisition was the most complex, took the most time and ultimately added the most value to our franchise. It was an acquisition that no one else could have done and in the seven years they had been trying to sell, no one else did.

Essex Bancorp was headquartered in Norfolk where we had always wanted to be. But they didn't have a branch there. They had their headquarters there and their loan sub-servicing operation there. Their actual branches were in Richmond (where they had two), Emporia, Suffolk and Elizabeth City, North Carolina.

We had a meeting with Essex's CEO, Gene Ross, after being introduced by Jake Savage, in the bar at TJ's in the Jefferson Hotel in Richmond in 2001. Essex Bancorp was too complicated. Nobody would ever buy it. It was an old thrift with a reasonably good deposit base. It had a loan sub-servicing company, which was the only thing that Gene Ross really cared about. It was a good business, but it was a business we just didn't understand. On the asset side they had a small builder construction loan business in their footprint and a big business in funding builder construction loans for three other originators outside their footprint. One of the three other originators was in Las Vegas. It was exactly the kind of thing that had gotten a lot of the old thrifts in trouble.

We told Gene that we loved the deposits, but that we didn't like the out of market construction lending and that we didn't understand the sub-servicing business at all. We told him that we'd be very interested in the branches and the deposits, but that we didn't want the rest. Gene was adamant about not splitting up the Bank and we amicably agreed to disagree.

THE IOS

Georgia: *The IOs were a serious crisis at a time when we were on a roll, but now everyone can laugh about it except for Rod and David.*

Rod: "IOs" are simply "Interest Only" strips from packages of loans or of loans that have been made into securities. When you buy them you don't own any of the principal balance of the loans. If the borrowers pay off the principal balance of the loans you stop getting the interest. That's bad. If the borrowers don't pay off the principal balance on the loans but keep paying the interest, that's good.

You buy residential mortgage IOs when you think rates are going up because borrowers tend not to refinance low rate mortgages in higher rate environments. If the borrowers don't refinance you keep getting the interest and your asset is worth more. Of course, the opposite is true. If you live by the sword, you die by the sword.

Let us take you back and explain why we bought the IOs in the first place.

Most of the time, markets are wonderfully efficient. Everyone knows all the relevant information. There are tens of thousands of men and women with more computing power than my father, who had access to the best military computers of the 1950's, ever dreamed of. They are staring at computer screens trying to make their employers rich by trading when a security price is minutely out of whack. They not only have more computing power than you do, they have more capital to commit than you do. You are beating your head against the wall if you try to trade against them.

If you've been around for several decades like David deGive and I have, there are a few times when you know more than the army of MBAs, techies and just plain nerds do.

The Spring of 2000 was one of those times. We'd watched the dotcoms and the technology stocks wax fat. We'd listened to all of the insanity that had infected a lot of our small-business customers. David, although I don't think he would admit it today, had even bought some tech stocks. As for me, while I wouldn't ever *buy* a tech stock; I would have liked to have *been* one. I regularly referred people to the classic *Extraordinary Popular Delusions and the Madness of Crowds*, by Charles Mackay. When a great book called Tulipomania, by Mike Dash, came out I recommended that as well. Ultimately, I don't think anyone paid any attention to either book. If they had no one would have ever bought any tech stocks. Some of you reading this today are feeling your toes and fingers curl up in fury and will throw down this book because your belief system has been violated. Calm down! The tech bubble was stupid, but it had extraordinary historical precedent, well documented in the above books.

The most recent precedent, however, was in Japan in the late 1980's. Japan convinced itself that the dynamics of "Japan Inc." were different from the rest of the world. In retrospect there were good things about Japanese business and there still are. There were a lot of good things about tulips. They were good for Holland's economy and they still are. However, the good things about Japanese business didn't justify the stocks of Japanese companies trading at 50, 60 or 70 price/earnings multiples while US companies traded at multiples in the 10s and 20s. It was insanity when the market capitalization of all the companies listed on the Tokyo Stock Exchange exceeded the market capitalization of all of the companies listed on the New York Stock Exchange in 1989, however briefly. It was insane when my Japanese colleague and friend from the Long-Term Credit Bank of Japan told me in 1986 that the land under the Imperial Palace in Tokyo was worth more than Florida! Georgia and I have run around the Imperial Palace and we've run around Palm Beach. We'll take Palm Beach. Forget the rest of Florida.

Regarding the IOs, it was insane when the Nikkei index peaked at just under 29,000 at the end of 1989. When the bubble burst it was more cataclysmic than anyone expected. Interest rates in Japan went into an extended swan dive and remained low for many, many years in Japan.

David deGive and I talked about it a lot in the Spring of 2000. In our gut we believed that something similar would happen in the US, a little more than a decade later, because a fundamental belief system had been shattered just as it has been in Japan. We were right. The experience in the US wound up being similar to what happened in Japan a decade earlier.

With the approval of the Board we acted on that belief. We lengthened the maturity of our portfolio and increased the size of the portfolio. We made tons of money for Southern Financial in both net interest income and gain on sale of sales of securities in 2000, 2001 and the Spring of 2002. In early 2002 I started getting goosey. I'm a firm believer in the US economy in the long run. I didn't want to be holding the bag if the economy bounced back and there was a reversal in interest rates. An unexpected, immediate upward shift in the yield curve of 200 basis points would have been unacceptably costly. We had big unrealized gains in the securities portfolio that we really didn't want to take all at once for cosmetic reasons. We started the process of trying to see how we could hedge ourselves.

Over the period of several months we looked at all of the options. The only really good one was to sell our appreciated securities and take our gains now. The cosmetics of that option were bad. We'd have a one-time gain now and, going forward, diminished net interest income. Moreover we didn't believe that an immediate rise in interest rates was probable — and indeed the Federal Funds rate wasn't hiked until mid-2004.

The steep yield curve made conventional hedging with interest rate swaps prohibitively expensive, although we were able to do some modest extensions of our funding. Our plan was ultimately to shrink our securities portfolio as we grew our loan portfolio to replace it.

We did add a small hedge. We bought about $11 million worth of residential mortgage IOs. Our reasoning was that if interest rates rose we'd lose some of the unrealized gains on our portfolio, but we'd make money on the IOs. It didn't seem like a big bet for a $400 million securities portfolio.

Georgia: *In September 2002 Bank has just hit the $1 billion mark and was hitting the ball out of the park on earnings.* (**Rod:** *A lot of the earnings were from our securities portfolio!*) *We just completed the Metro-County Bank acquisition. We had 27 branches and an incredible footprint. We had six analysts following us, with quarterly analyst conference calls, making earnings estimates and beating them. The market was finally buying our story. Our stock was on a roll.*

Rod and I were about to leave for a short vacation in Capri, one of our favorite places in the world. The day before we were scheduled to leave Trish Ferrick came into my office and said we have a situation with some of the IOs. Some of them were underwater and the accounting was completely different from the accounting for other mortgage-backed securities. They had to be marked to market through the income statement. I immediately called Rod. He said he didn't think the accounting made sense and that we should call Robert Best, our Partner at KPMG. We agreed on a conference call the next morning at 9:00 am.

So there we were on September 11th, the first anniversary of 9/11, on our way to Europe, with another crisis. On the conference call with Robert, Rod explained why he didn't believe that the write-downs were justified. Robert said that this was all new ground to him, that he would talk to the KPMG experts in this field and get back to us.

The train to Newark Airport was nearly empty, this being September 11th. Rod used the time on the train to call his friends in Wall Street to assess how big a problem the IOs could be. He was on the phone when Cary Morris, the bank analyst from Legg Mason walked by. We chatted with him about our trip to Capri and how everything was great. Afterward I told Rod we'd have to be more careful about talking on the cell phone.

By the time we got to Newark Airport we were experts in accounting for IOs and in how the pricing models worked. After we checked into the Alitalia lounge Rod talked to Steve Joseph who'd been looking at our IOs all day.

Rod: Steve confirmed that we had a Class A problem. The IOs we owned were ones that would perform best in a rising rate environment. They were also the ones that could be expected to perform the worst in a falling rate environment. There weren't any real bids in the street for them. The problem was that the coupons on the underlying mortgages of our IOs were primarily 5%. This was the beginning of a huge and completely unprecedented refinancing boom. The pricing models that determined how much our IOs were worth all used CPRs (Constant Prepayment Rates) to determine how quickly the mortgages underlying the securities we owned were being refinanced. The world was used to CPRs at 10% to 20%. In August they shot up to 40% and 50%. No one had any idea where they could go. It was unplowed ground — and a grim picture.

Georgia: *Rod was upset when he got off the phone with Steve. We strategized in the lounge and then later on the plane. We needed a worst-case scenario. Rod suggested that we put together a team to write a model to analyze what it could cost us over the next couple of quarters, given various assumptions as to prepayment speeds. That team was to be comprised of Trish Ferrick, Arlene Herlig and David deGive.*

I felt a little better since I thought we could get our arms around the problem. Little did I know...

When we got to our hotel we sent a message to the team and asked them to call us the next day at 9:00 am their time. We emphasized to them how important it was that we know how big the losses could be so we could plan our balance sheet strategy over the coming quarters. The three of them worked the whole weekend. For the next five or six days we got up in the morning and the desk clerk at La Scalinatella handed us a ream of faxes accumulated overnight — and I got depressed at the extent of the possible losses.

Rod: I have to mention that La Scalinatella is one of the best hotels in the world, though it's very small. They don't expect to receive 50 or 60 pages every morning with printouts of our IO models from Arlene.

Our dilemma was that we had substantial unrealized gains in other parts of our securities and loan portfolio. Except for the peculiarities of IO accounting the gains on the other securities would have largely offset the losses on the IOs. But we actually had to sell the securities and recognize the gains to offset the losses on the IOs. We hated selling the securities where we had gains because it adversely affected future period earnings.

Georgia: *One morning I couldn't handle it anymore and left Rod and took a walk down the Via Tragara. It is one of the most gorgeous walks in the world. I was in this beautiful place in tears. I kept thinking that David and Rod had really screwed up the Bank and there was absolutely nothing I could do. I finally calmed down and told myself that we needed to keep working on the problem until we understood how big it was.*

Rod: We began a process that was to last for several months. Our team built models and we continually reviewed and forecasted CPRs to decide what we'd sell to offset our losses. But this was uncharted water. No one could possibly know what was going to happen to CPRs. It was the worst possible problem for Georgia, who has an awful time handling uncertainty.

Georgia: *I returned to the hotel somewhat calmer but still upset. We returned home on September 24th really not rested. Based on our models at the end of the quarter we came to the conclusion that we were going to have a $2.5 million loss on the IOs for the third quarter. We were able to offset that loss with securities gains. We beat the analysts' estimates for the quarter, but Rod had to explain in our conference call what had happened. I didn't envy him, but he did superbly.*

He told the analysts, "Here's why we bought the IOs. We thought rates were going to rise and we needed to hedge. We still believe rates will rise. However, in hindsight we were clearly too early. We made a mistake." The analysts loved it. Much to my amazement they didn't beat him up. They didn't even ask him whether we had any more IOs, which we did. At that point we truly believed we'd taken our lumps.

However, it wasn't until the first quarter of 2002 when we finally finished all of our hits on the IOs. By then we'd written off nearly $9 million. To be sure, we had income on the other side, but it wasn't fun.

Finally, at the first quarter conference call for 2002, Rod began by saying, "I have two things to report today. First, Southern Financial Bank no longer owns any IOs. Second, and more importantly, Georgia and I are still married." It got a huge laugh. The analysts were impressed that when we made a mistake we admitted it and fixed it.

Essex Bancorp

Rod: In November 2002, a year after our last meeting with Gene Ross of Essex Bancorp, we were at the Sandler O'Neill Investor Conference at the PGA West, near Palm Beach.

Georgia: *We made a presentation that went really well. One of our large investors asked Rod about the IOs and whether he planned to buy any more. I immediately pulled the microphone away and said that Rod would not be able to buy any more IOs. That also got a big laugh. The husband/wife team aspect of our partnership was unique and we were Wall Street darlings, at least for a while.*

Rod: After our presentation, totally by accident, we end up at lunch with Tim Matz, of Elias Matz, whom we knew; and Harry Radcliffe, the largest shareholder of Essex. After lunch we caucused outside the dining room in the hall with Tim and Harry. We told Harry how interested we were in Essex and what our reservations were. He urged us to resume a dialogue with Gene Ross. He'd seen our presentation and liked what he'd heard.

A couple of weeks later we had another meeting with Gene, again at the Jefferson, but this time in the Washington Room. (If you pay for coffee and cookies you get to use that space for free). As is often the case in a merger the "social issues" were most critical. Loan Care, their sub-servicing company, was the ninth largest loan sub-servicer in the country. It was a profitable little operation, but it would be a sideshow for us and a business we just didn't understand. Gene understood it and loved it — still does. He built it from nothing. He would disagree but he wasn't particularly interested in Essex's other businesses. Gene basically didn't want to be involved with anything except Loan Care, which was fine with us.

At the meeting I proposed a spin-off of Loan Care to Essex shareholders with Southern Financial retaining 24.9% of the stock. Our interest was to keep Loan Care's escrow balances of nearly $100 million in Elisabeth City, North Carolina, which Southern Financial critically needed.

Everyone ultimately agreed on this structure and it was the basis on which the deal ultimately closed, but not until much later.

CHAPTER FOUR
THE ENDGAME

The Endgame

Rod: The endgame was absolutely awful.

It began with a call from Tom Grantham in February 2003. He'd been contacted by Alan Drewer from First Horizon, a mortgage company in Northern Virginia that was a subsidiary of First Tennessee National Corporation (FTN, its ticker symbol). Drewer told Grantham that FTN would like to talk with us. We told Tom that it sounded like amateur hour. We have always talked to everyone who wanted to talk to us. We answer our own phones and we answer our own voicemail. We told him to call one of us directly if they were serious.

We didn't know it then, but the endgame had begun. It extended over the next 11 months, but except for Drewer's telephone call to Tom Grantham, no one else in the Bank (besides Devon) on the Board of Directors knew anything at all about what was going on. There were absolutely no leaks because nobody but us knew anything to leak. When things heated up in the Spring we started spending a lot of our time in our offices in Georgetown. We let it be known that we enjoyed spending time at our townhouse. That was true, but another factor was that in Georgetown we ran significantly less risk of anyone overhearing a conversation they shouldn't hear.

A week or 10 days after Drewer's call to Tom Grantham, we got a call from Gerry Baker who ran First Horizon Mortgage nationwide for FTN Corp. We talked on the phone for about an hour. I was absolutely obnoxious to him and I did not believe there was any synergy between Southern Financial and a mortgage banking company whatsoever. I told him that we were a commercial bank that had largely exited the residential mortgage banking business to concentrate on small- and middle-market businesses. I tried again and again to explain why there was no potential for cross selling between a mortgage company and a commercial bank in our defined business segment.

Georgia: *I can honestly say that I never heard Rod so arrogant — and that's saying something — but Gerry was persistent.*

Rod: He would tell me that we could offer our small business owners financial planning and mutual funds. I would tell him that our small business owners had no liquidity, that they had all of their money invested in their businesses. Most of them really wouldn't have any liquidity until they sold their business. Otherwise they'd be rich enough to need real asset management, not financial planning from some kid with a new license. Then he'd say we can offer them home equity lines. I'd then tell him we already had seconds on their houses.

He finally wore me down and we agreed to meet with him and his CEO, Ken Glass, in Georgetown. We met on March 24th in our Georgetown office conference room. We were ultimately to have a couple of dozen meetings there with various suitors because it was a venue where our meetings didn't attract any attention.

We liked Ken Glass a lot. He was not a banker, but he explained his strategic need to grow his commercial banking business outside Tennessee, their home state where they are dominate major markets. FTN's non-banking businesses were too big and were threatening to overwhelm their basic banking operation. We agreed to visit them in Memphis.

We stopped in Memphis on the 15th and 16th of April on our way back from a weekend on the Georgia Bear in Palm Beach. We stayed in the wonderful Peabody Hotel — absolutely the best thing in Memphis — and spent a full day meeting with various people at FTN.

Georgia: *I loved the Peabody Hotel and enjoyed meeting the people at FTN, but the high point of the day came at 5 pm when the ducks crossed the lobby of the Peabody. For those of you who haven't been there it's an event not to be missed.*

Rod: Between our meeting in Georgetown and our arrival in Memphis we had done our homework on FTN. It was an intriguing company that was really quite different from other regional banks their size. The holding company had total assets of just over $25 billion at the end of 2003. In the first quarter of 2004 they had earnings of $119 million. It would make an excellent Harvard Business School case.

FTN was comprised of three completely different businesses.

- First, the commercial bank, First Tennessee Bank, which was 139 years old. We were a young institution but respectful of the fact that you don't get to be that old by doing things wrong. From the outside it appeared to be a strong, competent commercial bank. It did business in much the same way we did. We met several of their senior commercial bankers and were impressed. They spoke our language and we theirs. It was clear that they needed to move beyond Tennessee where they had very large market shares in most of their key markets. Banks love to talk market share, but there are points of diminishing returns. Our gut was they were hitting theirs.
- Second, they owned an excellent Investment Bank specializing in fixed income securities, First Tennessee Capital Markets. We were already a client of the Capital Markets group and didn't have to be convinced of how good they were. We had lunch with the head guy while we were in Memphis and continued to be impressed. (You may wonder why a major fixed income trading operation would be located in Memphis and not New York or Chicago. Memphis has been a fixed income trading center for decades. The entire trading apparatus for trading SBA loans has always been located there. I'm not sure why.)
- Third, they had a residential mortgage and consumer lending company called First Horizon Mortgage, which as relatively new and has been growing explosively nationally. They'd brought Gerry Baker in a couple of years earlier. His arrival coincided with a sustained decline in interest rates and a concomitant explosion in refinancings and new mortgage originations. He was bringing incredible amounts of earnings to FTN's bottom line. Their mortgage banking operation had gross earnings (pre-tax) of $100 million in the first quarter of 2004. The bank equity analysts were justifiably skeptical of those earnings and the street had punished FTN with a lower P/E multiple than its peer group.

When we visited Memphis we were already convinced that FTN was a terrific company with enormous potential and high-quality people. However, FTN's core problem was that not only was it split into three businesses, but that each of the three businesses had a different culture, with each being fundamentally dismissive of the other two.

Ken Glass had the advantage and disadvantage of not being from any of the three cultures. He was a complete outsider who'd become CEO in October 2001 and had been with the company since 1995. In theory he could mediate. But could he lead? Only time would tell.

Ultimately, the real dilemma for Georgia and me and for our shareholders was that any sale of Southern Financial would be paid for primarily in the stock of the acquirer. Most of our shareholders, including us, had a very low tax basis in our stock because we'd bought it many years earlier and it had gone up so much. None of us wanted to incur the tax consequences of selling the stock now or getting paid entirely in cash — though any deal generally includes some cash component. As a consequence, in any sale it's not just the ostensible price as calculated at the time of the announcement. Much more importantly, Georgia and I and our Board of Directors would have to make a judgement as to how the stock price of the acquirer would perform over time. With FTN that would be much more difficult than it would have been with a plain vanilla, large regional commercial bank.

They flew us back to Dulles. (Their airplane was the best! Georgia would never let me buy an airplane.) They'd promised to come up with an indicative range.

Georgia: *This was a crucial turning point for us. We had talked to a lot of potential acquirers over the years, but this was a terrific company even with the caveats. We had said for at least 10 years that we were for sale at the right price in the right currency, but no suitor had been as persistent as this one and we hadn't admired any of our suitors as much as we admired this one. We knew that we had a responsibility to our shareholders, including ourselves, to evaluate this seriously.*

We talked at length. The past year had not been fun. We had the IO crisis, a normal but stressful Federal Reserve exam and Sarbanes/Oxley. The compensation system that served us so well for so long was being questioned. Not only did we have a fiduciary responsibility to consider an offer, but when we thought it over we wanted an offer. Whether this was the right one and whether the price was right was another question. Whether this was a stock we and our shareholders would want to own for the long haul was yet another judgment we would have to make.

Rod: I think there was another factor at work here. Georgia and I can't say we aren't gamblers. In 1985 Georgia had given up a $100,000 a year job to roll the dice as an entrepreneur. At that point we'd put *all* of our chips on the table. We were working without a net.

Several years before that Georgia and I had a pre-honeymoon in Aruba. One night we stopped in the hotel casino. We bought $20 worth of chips and sat down at the roulette wheel. On the third or fourth spin we scored. We were up $30. I looked at her and said let's leave. She was probably the only woman in the world who would have agreed. The croupier was aghast. He said, "You can't do that." But we did.

We were at that same point psychologically in 2003. Maybe we can keep our chips on the table for another 10 years and make $50 to $250 million or lose it all. But in 10 years we'll be 70 years old. What would we do with $250 million then?

Unless you are obsessed, there is a point when you take your chips off the table and do something else. Maybe this is the point for us to cash in our chips in this glorious game we have been playing.

When It Rains it Pours

Back in our Georgetown office we got a call from an investment banker who asked whether we would like to meet with Kel Landis, the CEO of RBC Centura, the operating arm of the Royal Bank of Canada in the US. The Royal Bank of Canada is one of the 69 banks that dominate banking in Canada. It bought Centura Bank in January of 2001 and had made no secret of its intention to expand its banking franchise in the US. They already had some US assets in

2003, and they had already moved as close to us as Norfolk. We said we would meet with Kel, but that it had better be quick.

Kel came to see us in Georgetown on May 15, 2003. We talked in our conference room and then had dinner with him and several of his colleagues, including Royal Bank's Vice Chairman Jim Rager, at Café Milano. We liked Kel and Jim a lot, and it was clear we should visit Royal Bank's main office in Toronto as soon as possible.

Georgia and I called Gerry Baker at FTN and told him that we'd been approached by another bank and didn't know where it would lead, but that we'd see it through. We would follow parallel tracks with both banks. Gerry wasn't happy, but he went along with it.

Georgia: *We spent the weekend of June 7th and 8th in Connecticut and Harrison, New York. My sister June had her 50th birthday party.*

On Monday the 9th we went to New York to meet with Sandler O'Neill. Jimmy Dunne took us to P.J. Clarke's for lunch. Jimmy told us to proceed slowly, which was good advice. We asked him to detail Tom Duke to support us for the next couple of weeks, which he did.

Rod: That afternoon RBC flew Georgia, me and Tom Duke from New York to Montreal in Kel's plane — which was also fantastic! — at the height in Montreal's SARS epidemic. We had dinner in Royal Bank's executive dining room that night with Kel and Jim Rager. It was just the five or six of us on the top floor of their skyscraper overlooking the lake.

The next morning Georgia and I ran from the Royal York Hotel down to and along the lake.

At 9:00 am we met with a broad selection of Royal Bank's senior people. It was a full-court press designed to make us want to be a part of the Royal Bank. It worked on me more than Georgia. I thought Jim Rager, who was as committed to their technology as I was to ours, was wonderful. I had told him what we were doing with ARTS/WebLockBox and he told me about their retail marketing platform, which was absolutely state of the art. More importantly he took

The Endgame

Georgia and me down to the platform of their main branch and had various retail people give us live demonstrations. That was something I would have done in his position and it impressed me. He was the Vice Chairman of a several-billion-dollar bank and he knew how things worked and loved every inch of the business. An absolutely world-class guy. I was sold.

As I write this 14 months later, I'm a lot richer than I would have been had we sold to RBC, but I regret not being associated with this wonderful institution. Their CEO, Gordon Nixon, joined us for lunch and he was a marvelously charismatic guy. Ironically, like Ken Glass, he wasn't a banker either. He'd come up from the Investment Banking side of the house. When he finished lunch, he told the deal guys, "Don't screw this up!" They ultimately did, but his heart was in the right place.

There was a beautiful geographic fit with Centura Bank and an excellent business fit. Their stock was not going to skyrocket, but it was one we would like to own for the next 30 years. Importantly, we felt they would need all of our people.

The only problem was that they were not going to use an investment banker. They were going to use one of the people in their internal investment banking group. I had known him at Morgan Stanley where he was a Capital Markets guy — an excellent one, but not an investment banker.

Georgia: *Tom Duke of Sandler O'Neill maintained contact with them. A week and a half later, with us holding off FTN, Royal Bank came up with a range that was ridiculous. Six hours later they increased their range to match what FTN ultimately came up with. The numbers all worked. They would have made us and our other shareholders very happy. But we were uncomfortable with the process. We felt that we were on the block. As ridiculous as it sounds, something didn't feel right. I remembered Jimmy Dunne's advice, "Go slow!"*

My baby just deserved better. We were flattered with the intense interest, but hadn't been comfortable with the process. We ultimately didn't feel that the indicative ranges, which were very close to each other, reflected the value of our franchise.

We had Tom Duke call both FTN and Royal Bank and declined to continue our discussions. We thanked both of them for their interest. We were out of the game. It was a relief.

We spent the next several weeks trying to run the Bank and get the Essex deal closed.

The End of the End Game

On August 26, 2003, Fulton Bankshares announced its purchase of Resource Bankshares in Norfolk at an incredibly high price, and Fulton's stock did not go down. The world changed for us forever. All of a sudden Southern Financial was the only significant franchise left in Virginia's urban/suburban non-rural markets. It was something we had been working toward for years, but it sort of happened all at once. Three mid-Atlantic bank CEOs called us within days and scheduled meetings.

We asked Jimmy Dunne to have his people review all of our Mid-Atlantic options, plus FTN and RBC Centura. This time we wanted to control the process. This was going to be the most important decision we would make in our lives. We wanted to make sure that we would make it based on all of the very best information and analysis. Sandler O'Neill put its investment bankers, its analysts and its data bases to work, to prepare for a meeting in late September.

We had the meeting in the Fredericksburg on September 23rd. Only Tom Duke made it with the books. Jimmy Dunne and Emmett Daley had their plane cancelled, but they were on the speaker phone.

We ended up with a short list of potential buyers. Ironically, of the short listers, Gary Geisel, Rufus Fulton, and Richard Adams had already scheduled meetings with us. Ned Kelly had not, but Jimmy took care of that immediately.

We had a series of four lunches with our suitors. To put everyone on the same footing, all four were at the Bistro Francais on M Street — a Georgetown fixture since 1975 — at the back table where we always ate. It was private and we did not have to think about what to have. I always had the steak Caesar rare and Georgia has the regular Caesar. The Bistro Francais is a Georgetown fixture.

The Endgame

We'd already had a meeting with Gary Geisel on the 19th. He managed to convey intensity with a feeling that he listens. As with the others that were to follow, we talked through our strategy and he talked through his. He kept emphasizing how a Southern Financial merger would advance all of the strategic objectives that he had outlined with the bank equity analysts. He was totally credible. As we ended lunch he said that if we were ever interested in pursuing a combination to give him a call. We said that the time was now if he was interested. He got back to us the next day. We agreed to come up to Baltimore and meet with Kevin Byrnes, his COO, and Dennis Starlipper, his CFO. Gary was the consensus manager and for better or worse the three of them really ran the bank together.

Our next meeting was with Rufus Fulton and Charles Nugent on September 26th. We had a cordial lunch at the Bistro. They were a multibank holding company. They had just bought Resource Bankshares in Norfolk and were committed to having Resource remain independently managed. As you will recall it was a business model we fervently do not believe in.

They suggested that Southern Financial could keep its name. Rufus said that we would continue to run the Bank. Georgia asked what that would involve. Rufus answered some credit decisions, no investment decisions, no capital worries, keep our own Board in place, budgets and regulators. We said that if we wanted to continue running the Bank we would wait five years and then buy *them*. (**Georgia:** *A bit of Rod arrogance!*) Rufus did not listen and continued doggedly ahead.

Georgia: *He told me, "Once a year all the CEO's get together with spouses for a weekend to exchange ideas and play golf."* (**Rod:** *I would get to come too!*) *It sounded like a junior varsity VBA meeting that we had never attended. Rufus added that that year's outing would be in Princeton, New Jersey. There's nothing wrong with Princeton, but spending a weekend with people you don't really have anything in common with except a holding company is not my idea of fun. I would prefer to spend the weekend alone with Rod on an island and bounce ideas off him. (Rod, don't let that go to your head!)*

Rod: At that point I looked at Georgia and almost laughed. I knew any Fulton deal was stillborn from that point on. We walked back together to our offices.

Rufus walked with Georgia and Charles walked with me. Charles seemed to have sensed that it hadn't gone at all well and was trying for a stick save. It didn't work and Rufus did no better with Georgia.

Richard Adams of United Bankshares was next, on October 2nd. We knew more about United than any of the others. We'd watched them make a series of acquisitions in Virginia, Maryland and DC, which have transformed them from a sleepy West Virginia bank to a Mid-Atlantic banking power, with more than half their assets outside their home state. Our only criticism of them was that they were a laggard in technology.

We had met Steve Wilson, the CFO, probably 10 years earlier when United first embarked on its acquisition effort in Virginia. However, until our lunch in the Bistro Francais, we'd never met Richard Adams. Richard turned out to be intense — not a Jimmy-Dunne level, but close — and charismatic. We loved the fact that he and his family owned 600,000 shares of United's stock. He was also an autocratic manager — although not at the Georgia level. Richard had spearheaded the series of acquisitions responsible for United's growth. A Southern Financial purchase would have been a very important additional step in that strategy. Southern Financial would have been their largest acquisition. They could achieve economies by closing some Southern Financial and/or United branches where there was an overlap. The stakes were very high for Richard and we sensed United would be aggressive.

Finally, we met with Ned Kelly, the new CEO of Baltimore's Mercantile Bank Shares, on September 29th and then went up to meet with him in Baltimore again on October 14th. Ned, who was from Davis Polk and J.P. Morgan, took over Mercantile from Henry Furlong Baldwin, known to everyone as "Baldy," about three years earlier. We had immensely more in common with Ned than any other CEO we had ever met. He had enough self confidence in himself to have fun. He wore perfect English tailored suits and at our first meeting had a Turnbull and Asser tie. I had a Turnbull and Asser shirt, and I teased him about his tie, telling him that Jimmy Dunne had said that was what he would be wearing. He owned a farm in Charlottesville where he stayed every weekend. (The only place more pretentious than Charlottesville is The Plains, where we have our farm.) Our two meetings with Ned were immense fun.

Ned had made his first acquisition post "Baldy" about six months earlier and his stock had been creamed on day one, about 13%. At our first meeting he said he didn't think he would do another acquisition until the first or second quarter of 2004. We said we understood and mentally crossed Ned off the list. We told Jimmy, and he said to put him back on.

By the 15th of October the train was leaving the station. We decided to allow United, Provident and Mercantile to do preliminary due diligence. Jimmy put Emmett Daley in charge of the process, from the Sandler O'Neill side. We brought Rick Steele into the loop. It was his job to help us assemble the due diligence materials.

Rick, Georgia and I assembled the due diligence materials without anyone else knowing. Rick, who is among other things, Corporate Secretary, went to Warrenton at night and on the weekend and assembled boxes of critical information. Georgia got updated budgets from Trish, and I printed out all of Bill Stevens' loan reviews.

We set up an off-site due diligence room in a hotel on Route 7 in Tyson's Corner.

The drill was that each bank sent in a team to review the material we had assembled. United's team came in on the 16th and 17th of October, Provident's on the 20th and 21st and Mercantile's on the 22nd and 23rd. Rick was there everyday with someone from Sandler O'Neill almost every day. Georgia and I met with each team on the first day and then answered questions for a couple of hours on the final day.

The United Bank team was the most professional. United's CFO led the team and the fact that they had 26 acquisitions under their belt showed. Their team was a well-oiled machine. They focused on all the right things. They were thorough and tough.

Provident came next. We worried that they were trying to be so nice to us that they were not going to dig deep enough.

Mercantile was an absolute circus. They had at least six Davis Polk lawyers, two investment bankers from J.P. Morgan and at least two dozen others who we presumed were with Mercantile.

We had our regular board meeting on Thursday the 23rd, which was Mercantile's second day of preliminary due diligence. Of our directors only Neil Call knew anything was going on. It was surreal. Adding to the pressure on Georgia, Bill Stevens, our EVP of Risk Management, forgot that the meeting was in Georgetown and went to Warrenton. He missed the audit committee meeting, which he was supposed to chair. (He was often a parody of himself.) The board meeting started with a presentation from a Vice President and two other officials from the Richmond Fed to review the exam we had in the spring.

Ironically this was the first time anyone from the Fed had attended one of our board meetings, ever. They were complimentary concerning our response to the exam. Afterward one of our directors said, "I thought they were very nice." Georgia and I wished he had the opportunity to meet them during the exam.

The board then reviewed and approved our 3Q03 earnings release, which was strong, but I found my attention wandering. I gazed out the window. After the meeting we briefed Bob Warhurst, to bring a third director in the loop.

We left the board meeting to drive over to Tyson's Corner to the Mercantile Bank due diligence bonanza. We spent about two hours answering questions.

The next morning we reconvened in Georgetown for our quarterly analyst conference call with Trish, who knew nothing, and Rick, who knew everything and was beginning to show the strains. The conference call was generally excellent with around 30 analysts and investors on the line.

Georgia and I started the weekend as two very tired puppies.

On Monday we tried to run the Bank a little before taking the train to New York on Tuesday. Final indications were due later that day and the plan was to meet with Jimmy and the other Sandler O'Neill people and to evaluate the bids on Wednesday. When we got to the Peninsula Hotel we called Emmett at around 5 pm. Emmett told us that he had indications from United and Provident, which were for all practical purposes identical. Mercantile decided not to bid. The bids were above their original indications and about $6 a share higher than the indications from FTN and RBC, which started this whole process. We were at once euphoric and scared to death.

Georgia: *The next morning before we went to Sandler O'Neill's office I had a three-hour Board conference call with Oneida Ltd., where I was still on the Board. Needless to say, my mind was not on Oneida.*

Rod: Before we arrived at Sandler O'Neill I decided United was the one. We spent several hours with Jimmy, Emmett and others analyzing the bids. It was clear that both United and Provident felt they had to do a pre-emptive bid and both did. During the meeting I changed my mind and by the time we left Sandler O'Neill I began leaning toward Provident.

At that point our focus was on the bidder. Which one had executed better over the past five years? Whose core business model was better? Whose demographics were better? Which one did Southern Financial make better? Which one really needed us most? Most importantly, which stock would we and our other shareholders want to own? They were not easy questions to answer, since the two banks were so different.

We left Sandler O'Neill still undecided and wandered Manhattan for a couple of hours before ending up in a Chinese restaurant next to my old apartment on 56th street. Georgia was totally upset. This was her baby. She was 18 and it was time for her to leave the house and get married — but to whom? We continued the debate.

Georgia: *The next morning we were going to take the Acela back to Washington. We were both emotional basket cases. In the Acela lounge at Penn Station we called Emmett, who has been a Provident supporter since the beginning. We asked him whether or not Gary could execute this deal.*

I asked him how long had Gary been running Provident. Emmett said for 12 years, which was not true. Peter Martin had run Provident until nine months earlier. It was a weird statement that colored the way I thought about everything Emmett said thereafter.

We told Emmett that we had not made up our minds yet. We were having a bad case of seller's remorse. I really wanted a reason to choose United because I thought Richard Adams was so good.

On the train came the moment I had dreaded the most: I had to tell my people what was going on. One by one I called Bill Stevens, Bill Lagos, Jackie Fitterer, Mary Ellen Clancy and Trisha Ferrick. David deGive already knew. I scheduled a conference at 2:00 pm. It was then that I told them that we had received several offers and that we were about to accept one of them, and that we needed all of them to work that coming weekend. I promised them that we would compensate them, but that was probably the last thing on any of their minds. They all responded like the consummate professionals they were.

Back in our Georgetown offices, we got a call from Jimmy. (I wish I could quote Jimmy's lines verbatim because I would be rich. I will try to get them as close as I can.)

Jimmy: "How are you doing?"

Georgia: "Awful."

Jimmy: "Yeah. I talked to Emmett, who said that you were really intense. I told him that Georgia built this Bank with her bare hands over the past 20 years and I would be worried if Georgia was not upset."

We talked some more to Jimmy. Putting all the analysis aside it came down to two simple things. First, the map with Provident was better — a better deposit franchise. They were where anyone in their right mind wanted to be. With our branches they would be even stronger. Second, if Gary executed the deal it would create a Mid-Atlantic powerhouse. If he didn't, someone else would buy them at a hopefully higher price, and it was a double dip.

We told Jimmy to tell Gary that we had picked Provident.

Rod: Final due diligence was in two groups. One in Vienna and one in Warrenton.

The Endgame

Georgia and I spent both days with Bill Stevens, Jackie Fitterer and Mary Ellen Clancy in Vienna.

Georgia: *Gary never appeared at the final due diligence. He stayed home all weekend. We'd never not been at a due diligence meeting. Rod and I always made it a point to be at final due diligence. There's nothing more important. But Gary never called me to ask how things were going. I began to question his social skills.*

Rod: On Sunday November 2nd we were wrapping up due diligence and discussing the final points of the definitive agreement. We had told them a week before that we didn't want to discuss issues relating to us on the last day, but they were there with a bombshell. This may be boring to you, but it wasn't to us.

Section 280 g of the Internal Revenue Code is simple: if you get paid an amount in connection with a merger, greater than three times the average of your past five years of earnings, you pay a punitive excise tax. Since most contracts require the buyer to indemnify you from the tax through grossing up your payment, buyers are very sensitive to this issue.

What generally happens is that the covered executives agree to tear up their contracts, and restructure everything to avoid the buyer having to pay the gross-up. Normally the pact includes a non-compete agreement, payable over several years, which would keep the executives of the seller from starting anew and taking business away from the buyer. It's extraordinarily logical and it works. Provident, through its attorneys, absolutely refused. One of their Muldoon Murphy lawyers said on the 2nd, "Why should we do that, just for your convenience?" He should have been fired then, but it turns out Provident doesn't fire anyone. So we didn't get a non-compete, even though it would have cost them nothing. (Only time will tell whether that was a catastrophic mistake on Provident's side. At the very least, if I were Gary I would never use Muldoon Murphy again.)

On November 3, 2003 we had the Board Meeting that would determine everything at 7:30 am in a conference room at Bracewell, Patterson in Reston. As usual Georgia and I were there an hour early and were standing at the front door when Emmett and the legal beagles arrived.

Georgia: *Emmett came up to me and said there was still one small item on the table. I asked him what. He said that Provident's lawyers were still concerned about the "pay for stay pool." In almost all bank deals there is a pool of money that helps the management of the selling institution keep it together until the deal closes. We'd offered one to all four banks we acquired. It had gone awry only once. Gary wanted to be able to approve all the payments. It was 10 minutes before our critical Board meeting. I was emotional and furious. Emmett hadn't served us well at all. It turned out to be a huge problem, but with 10 minutes to go there was nothing I could do.*

Rod: David deGive, Bob Warhurst, John Bellotti and Dick Smith all arrived before 7:15 am and we hooked up the speakerphone and tried to make small talk. Everyone had been on the phone on Friday except Alfonso Finochiaro, who had returned from Santo Domingo in the Dominican Republic on Sunday and had stayed awake all night reading the materials Sandler O'Neill and Bracewell had sent him. Alfonso was a dear friend and a valuable member of the SFB board. He'd already retired by this time.

One by one the other directors, except Virginia Jenkins, who was in Italy, called in. Everyone was solemn. Emmett took the floor and launched into his prepared presentation. One by one the directors began to question him. "Why now? Why not in three years?" "Why would we sell to a bank with a .70 efficiency ratio?" (Ours was .46 and lower is better.)

Alfonso in particular asked all the right questions and gave Emmett a thorough grilling. Emmett did not expect it and squirmed more than I thought he should have. He would have been richly compensated for 15 minutes of stress. In the end, the Directors voted unanimously to sign the definitive agreement, but for those of us in the Bracewell conference room, it felt like a wake. We sat around for a few minutes signing documents before we left. Dick Smith came up to us afterward openly crying. "I have been honored to serve on this board," Dick said. "It has been a learning experience."

Georgia: *We drove back to Warrenton after the Board meeting to participate in Provident's 10:30 am Analyst Conference call. "How badly is their stock going to be hit?" we thought. We almost missed the call. Rod took the wrong exit from 267* *to 28 and we ended up in a traffic jam on the way to Leesburg. We got to Warrenton at around 10:25 am. There were more than 75 participants on the call. I said a few words and Gary waxed eloquent. He was fine with Southern Financial's stock settling in at just over 43. Jimmy was too pessimistic.*

We'd tentatively set up a meeting on Wednesday afternoon for Provident to introduce themselves to Southern Financial's AVP's and above. We confirmed that while we were stuck in traffic. But we also told Gary that we wanted to meet with him before the mass meeting to talk about our loan officers and their credit support. Gary said fine and we said we'd meet him at the Bailiwick Inn, next door to our Fairfax City branch, at noon, just before the mass meeting.

After the conference call we called Claire's and invited everyone in Warrenton down to the Boardroom for lunch. Laura went out and bought a half dozen bottles of Korbel.

(**Rod:** Laura, its not Georgia's preferred brand! It tastes a little like bananas.) *We spent the rest of the afternoon with the old-timers, including Bertie, an honorary old-timer, reminiscing about what we'd been through. Some of the discussion was pretty scatological.*

Rod: Georgia and I had dinner at Tadpole's Cafe, which is the only place near the farm open on Mondays, and drove home to Marblehead Farm. We hadn't been there for weeks and our Bichons Frises and our Italian Springer Spaniel were batshit.

On Tuesday November 4th we were numb. We talked to a lot of our people. They cried. We cried. We received unbelievable coverage in *The Washington Post* and the *Washington Times*.

This is the day the enormity of it all settled atop of me. I talked to the people special to me. Jacques, Diane, Cristen, Michelle B, David, Dave, Alicia, Aidan, Devon, Carmelita and Shanna. Georgia talked to her group. I had nothing else to do in the afternoon and I took our car down to the carwash. That was the most fun of my day.

That night we ate dinner at the Rail Stop, which is our normal Tuesday place. When we got to the farm we drove up to Frank and Julia Woodson's, the couple who managed our farm, to see how Julia was doing. She was undergoing chemotherapy for liver cancer. Frank had quadruple bypass surgery a couple of years earlier, but was doing great and taking care of Julia, insisting on doing absolutely everything else on the farm. (Julia and Frank have run our farm for 18 years. I admire Frank immensely, but that's another book.)

Frank had dimmed the lights everywhere but in the kitchen. It was over 80 degrees in the house. Georgia went in the bedroom with Julia while Frank and I stood in the living room and talked guy talk about the tractors and bush hogs. Georgia massaged Julia's legs and fed her ice. "I love you honey. We're going to make it," Georgia said. She did make it.

Georgia: *We met Gary Geisel and Kevin Byrnes for lunch at the Bailiwick Inn on November 5th, before our meeting with the employees. We expressed our concern that if they handled it wrong they would destroy our engine of growth: our commercial lending department. That was our core strength that they were paying a handsome price for. We volunteered to travel to Baltimore the next day and talk through how they were organized and recommend a structure that would retain the best of both – and ensure that they don't have a mass exodus of our loan officers who were already getting headhunter calls. We also suggested that they consider granting our loan officers stock options immediately after closing. (They ultimately didn't until it was too late.)*

Kevin's immediate response was dogmatic. "We are organized the way we're organized and we're not going to change," he said. "You will fit your people into our three doors." He was also hostile to the idea of stock options for our people.

Rod: At one point during the lunch Georgia turned off. Georgia's people know what it means when Georgia gives you the "hairy eyeball." Georgia gave Kevin a third-degree hairy eyeball and suggested that it would be a waste of time for us to go to Baltimore tomorrow.

Gary, who is much more socially sensitive than Kevin, was conciliatory and insisted we go, which we did.

The Endgame

Georgia: *We took separate cars to drive back to the Best Western where their staff was to meet ours. I told Rod we'd made a horrible mistake. They were going to destroy everything I'd built.*

We walked into the Monticello Room in the Fairfax Best Western where we'd had a dozen Fairfax Advisory Board meetings. It was clear from the beginning that this was going to be different. From our side we had about 30 AVP's and above. We didn't have any more.

They had at least as many people as we did. It would become clear that we were culturally very different. They had one person per function. We had one person per multiple functions and were proud to the core of our beings for it. Later the reports from our people trickled in. They had 26 people working on their website. We had three-fourths that number of people and ours was better. They had 66 people in IT, including the 26 on their website, and we had three. We had two people in marketing and they had 26 and didn't produce a quarterly newsletter like we did.

I made a brave, upbeat introduction for the Provident people:

"This is an exciting time. Bitter sweet. On Monday we were sitting in the offices of Bracewell Patterson with our directors either on the phone or present, along with representatives of Bracewell Patterson and Emmett Daly from Sandler O'Neill. Emmett Daly was explaining the transaction, and then he said the purchase price is $330 million. I looked over at Rod and said, 'Wow, from '$4 million in capital to $330 million.' We have come a long way and guys from Southern Financial it's all because of you.

"Why have we been so successful? It's due to our enthusiasm, our energy, our 'can do' attitude. We were the little bank that could. How often we would go to customers offices and they would say, 'Who is Southern? We have never heard of you.' We responded: 'We can do anything you want. We will be more responsive and quicker. We can move fast but we are not going to be the cheapest. You pay for what you get.'

"Now, as some of you are going to work for Provident, and some of you are going somewhere else, I want you to embrace all those qualities that make us so successful, our enthusiasm, our energy and our excitement. As Linda Sandridge said,

'Southern Financial has unbridled enthusiasm,' and I ask you to take this with you wherever you go. These qualities will help you to move forward in a successful career.

"Some might ask, 'Why sell now?' Simply put, you sell when someone wants to buy you.

"'Why Provident?' Simply put, it is the map. Look at the location of our branches together with Provident. Together we could become a Mid-Atlantic banking powerhouse.

"Some of you might say I don't know what is going to happen tomorrow, I don't know what I will be doing. None of us know for sure what is going to happen. So relax and keep your enthusiasm, your energy and your 'can do' attitude."

Rod spoke next, and he finished by saying, "I would just like to say that Gary Geisel is the bravest CEO I've ever met – for inviting Georgia on his Board of Directors. She's never been known to suppress her opinions and I don't think she's going to start now."

Gary spoke next and he was excellent. He exuded sincerity and the Southern Financial staff accepted him. We haven't talked to anyone who didn't come away liking him. (Was he too nice? No one has ever accused me of that!)

Kevin spoke next and he grated — at least on me. He talked too long and he made the canned Provident speech, showing he hadn't listened to us at all. He said how cool Provident was since they'd had totally free checking since 1993. Later, I called him on the fact that he knew Southern had it since 1986, on day one, but hadn't thought to credit us. He lost a lot of hearts and minds on that one — including mine. He talked about Provident's bonus plan — Southern Financial's is immensely more lucrative for good performers. He hadn't listened and he had no clue.

Enos Frye spoke next and he was also excellent. Then Jean Uphouse, Provident's Head of the Human Resource Department, spoke mostly about the timetable. She said everyone would know by the end of February whether they would be offered a job and what that job would be. (The meetings with the HR "professionals" at the end of February were to be an unqualified disaster.)

The Endgame

There were questions after the Provident presentations. Jacques Smith asked one of the first and it was the ultimate, "Why is the Emperor not wearing any clothes?" question. Jacques asked, "You have 56 people in Information Technology and we have five, what do all of yours do?" Jacques charitably didn't add that we wrote all our own state of the art systems, ARTS, WebLockBox and Southern Cash Manager. They had done nothing *internally. They outsourced everything.*

Kevin shot back: "We're a much bigger bank and have a lot more accounts." His arithmetic didn't add up. Gary said, "I have no idea. Next question." It was a better answer, but unfortunately it was true. It was a defining moment. Gary never made an effort to get an answer to the question as far as I know. It would go a long way toward figuring out why Provident's efficiency ratio is in the mid-60's — a level that Dennis Starlipper acknowledges would give "you a nosebleed."

These responses to Jacques's question set the tone for the Southern Financial side's agonizing six months until the deal finally closed.

Rod: *On November 6th we woke early as usual and worked out. At 6:45 am Georgia started getting emails from Tom Grantham on her new Blackberry. She was doing her hair. I was nude and she wanted to talk. I offered an alternative that she declined.*

Georgia: *Tom was concerned about the previous night's meeting. He was worried about the vibrations, about what the deal will do to our loan officers' entrepreneurial spirit. All the loan officers are concerned about how Provident rigidly segments C&I loans, commercial mortgages and small business. None of our people do just one thing. Their people all do just one thing. That was to become the theme of the next couple of weeks. I emailed: "For those of you who are not bankers or loan officers this is no trivial issue. It was at the core of what we were. It was why we ate everyone else alive."*

Rod: *In Georgetown early, I talked with Dianne Smith, who headed our two-person but superb marketing department. She had spoken briefly the previous night with her counterpart in Provident's marketing department. In Georgetown Dianne asked if they had a newsletter, which they didn't. "We communicate to our customers in different ways," Provident's marketing associate said. "What do* all of your people do?" Dianne asked. "Each person has a single job to do," they answered.

You get a flavor here. Our people were Special Forces Operatives who were being absorbed by the regular Army supply corps. Maybe that is not a perfect analogy, but it's close enough.

Jimmy Dunne, the head of Sandler O'Neill, called us. He asked how things were going. We told him awful. Jimmy said, "You have to understand that you've sold your baby and there is going to be a period of mourning." Georgia said, "Bull, if they would just give us a check we're out of here. But they are going to screw up the people who were with us in the creation of this magnificent situation." We told Jimmy all about our lunch with Gary and Kevin, and about Kevin's dogmatic responses. Jimmy tried to make us feel better, but gave up after a while.

We then had a long drive on a desolate rainy day up to Baltimore. We parked in the third floor of Provident's new parking lot. Their elevator still didn't work and I gimped down to the ground floor.

We had told Gary we wanted to start with a two-on-one. He brought us back to his office. Kevin and Dennis were in their offices and we waved.

We said to Gary that he had promised to be frank and that we would, too. We told him we thought his speech the day before was good. But Kevin had not listened and he grated on our loan officers. We told Gary that if he allowed Kevin to continue direct contact with the loan officers that Provident would lose them and what they had bought would be totally hollowed out. Gary seemed to understand. He said that sometimes Kevin listened without seeming to. Georgia and I remained skeptical.

After meeting with Gary we walked down the corridor to their executive dining room and spent three hours with Kevin; Hugh Newton, Provident's Head of Commercial Banking; and Les Patrick, the company's Chief Credit Officer. Kevin was blissfully silent most of the time. We talked through their lending structure and ours, and the strengths of each and every one of our lenders. Provident was clearly segmented and held together with belts and suspenders and Southern Financial were not. You can make an argument for belts and suspenders: your pants do not fall off. The argument against, of course, is that it takes twice as long if you need to change your pants. Hopefully we'd made our case.

We drove back to Washington feeling better. About halfway there Georgia suddenly said, "Jimmy Dunne called them; they were cooperative." I said we would ask him when we see him next week.

The next day, Friday, we left for Palm Beach to attend the Sandler O'Neill conference at Palm Beach Gardens. We had presented the previous year and had been scheduled to present again, but given the pending sale there was nothing for us to say. We decided to go anyway and have the boat ride on the Georgia Bear, which we did the previous year, even though we had nothing to sell. We had already paid for the Breakers, for catering the lunch, and Linda Sandridge and Laura Vergot already had tickets to go down and assist in the festivities. It was not work this time; it was an unabashed boondoggle.

On Saturday morning Georgia and I went out for a jog and there was a 1950's, left-hand drive Bentley in the parking lot of the Brazilian Avenue Docks. It was identical to the one my father had bought in England several years before he died. He brought it back to Kentucky and it was his most prized possession.

After our run we stopped by Scotty's where we buy our wine and booze in Palm Beach. We needed some more things for the boat ride. At the last minute I thought that some of the guests would want beer and I turned toward the beer cooler. The first thing I saw was Grolsch with flip tops. My father used to have Grolsch delivered to our house when we lived in Holland. It was his favorite beer and he hated it when we returned to the US and could not buy it anymore.

Coincidences? A left-hand drive Bentley and flip-top Grolsch in the same morning? Maybe. But maybe my father was trying to tell me that he was there and that he was proud.

Linda and Laura arrived Monday. We had a marvelous week. Both of them were upset about the change that will inevitably result from the merger. But both of them have substantial stock options and will be at least modestly wealthy.

We went to great restaurants, jogged (not Linda), talked at length, drank several times immoderately and called everyone who would answer the phone. Linda, Laura and Georgia mounted several expeditions to Worth Avenue and brought gladness to the merchants there. They all bought designer sunglasses because I *hate* sunglasses.

Laura Vergot, Georgia and Linda Sandridge

I stocked up on socks at Brooks Brothers.

On Thursday we went to the Sandler O'Neill conference. We had lunch with Carl Palmer, an old Chemical banker. He is now President of Pointe Bank in Florida and talked with Alan Fishman, another Chemical alum who was also CEO of Independence Bank in Brooklyn. It was a day of high fives and congratulations.

We saw Jimmy Dunne, who was as feisty as ever. We asked whether he had called Gary Geisel last week. He admitted he had, but would not say anything else.

We sat in on Provident's presentation, given by Gary Geisel and Dennis Starlipper. It was OK. Gary was very nervous. We were sitting in the first row.

Georgia: We hadn't talked to Gary since the announcement of the deal. After their presentation we took Gary aside for a private talk. Gary admitted that he hadn't thought the presentation had gone well.

We also told him that we thought that he had been very badly served by his lawyers. They could have gotten us to execute a non-compete agreement at no cost to Provident and it would have been immensely helpful to us personally. He thanked us for our input.

Rod: The next day was our boat ride on the Georgia Bear. We had a wonderful time. We had nothing to sell. The group of about 10 investors just clicked and we had a marvelous discussion about various banks and different business models.

Linda and Laura left Saturday and returned to Virginia. That evening Georgia and I were having a glass of wine on the aft deck at dusk, just before dinner. A beautiful yacht about 90 feet long glided in behind us and entered the slip on the Australia dock opposite ours. It was a Leopard. It was only the second one we had ever seen — Herman Sandler's was the first. If Herman was trying to send us a congratulatory message that's how he'd have done it.

Georgia: After Palm Beach Rod and I flew off to Italy for two weeks and bought the house in Italy that we had been searching for for years. It's in Tropea, Calabria, in the toe of the boot near Sicily. Tropea is a pre-medieval walled city built on a rock on the coast with miles of white sandy beaches. Our house is an apartment in a 16th century convent built on Roman and Norman walls. We look out on the beaches, the Tyrrenian Sea and a 10th century church on an island. It's neat. We closed on the house on Thanksgiving Day.

Chapter Five
The Post Game

The Post Game

Rod: This book should have been over with the end of the last chapter. It would have been a great ending. But our most important insights about why Southern Financial had been so successful came after we returned from Italy after Thanksgiving — during the agonizing transition.

We were in touch with all parties via Blackberry and phone while we were gone. But when we got back there was a virtual flood of messages.

On Tuesday the 2nd of December I had lunch at the Bistro Francais with Diane Smith and Cristen Smith. It was absolutely gut wrenching. Diane, with Cristen's help, did our Annual Report, our quarterly newsletters, our advertising, our press releases, all of our brochures. They also did all of our mailings, everything the branches needed *and* they went out periodically to the branches to promote the products du jour. The quality of their work product was absolutely extraordinary.

They are married to brothers — both named Smith — and they live in Caroline County, which is south of Fredericksburg, nearly a two-hour drive from Warrenton. For a long time they commuted to and from Warrenton every day. Both of them have babies. Georgia and I admire them both incredibly.

I'd talked to Lillian Kilroy at the November 5th meeting. I asked her whether Provident had a newsletter. She said dismissively that they didn't, but that they "communicated with their customers in other ways." That was a completely asinine response for two reasons. First, on the retail side, Chevy Chase, which was Provident's major competitor for retail business, had a superb newsletter for its retail customers. It was our model. It was why Georgia finally let me use color. Second, we subsequently learned that Provident had a newsletter for its commercial customers produced by "Washington" — probably its Tyson's Corner office. We haven't seen it yet as we write this.

Lillian had spent most of a day with Diane and Cristen. They didn't tell me this, but when it was over they were devastated. She told them how she'd gotten a great deal on her Lexus. She also told them how much she liked their space in Breezewood. Diane was convinced that she was planning to throw them out and make it into a training center. The only role that she talked about for the two of them was to visit the branches and sell products.

Provident had 66 people in the marketing department. We had two. They outsourced much of what they did, including merger letters. We outsourced nothing. My biggest fight ever with Georgia was about putting our newsletters in color. If I had suggested that we pay someone outside the bank to write letters she would have fired me. And she would have been right.

(See Appendix I, SFB's Fall 1999 Newsletter discussing the Horizon Merger)

The next day, was absolutely critical for the Bank as well as Devon. Southern Financial was one of the finalists for an RFP bid for the Washington Metropolitan Airports Authority (MWAA). It would allow us to open a branch in each of Dulles and Reagan National airports and operate nearly 20 cash machines within the two of them. This was huge. Each of the airports was a small city. Dulles had 8,000 employees and National had 14,000. Dulles had a major domestic and international air cargo business; National, a wonderful shopping mall. Devon had been working on this proposal for several months and had invested his heart and soul in it.

As soon as the merger was announced, actually at the November 5th meeting, Devon had talked to Hugh Newton about the necessity for Provident to express its support of Southern Financial's bid. Hugh responded with enthusiasm. Now, Devon was one of several finalists to be invited back to present to the MWAA Committee, who would make the final decision. John King and Joan Welch from Provident had also agreed to come. I went because there was no way emotionally I couldn't. Georgia had to go to the dentist. (It turned out she had her wisdom tooth pulled while we were in the meeting.) She and I wanted this deal as badly as Devon did.

The Post Game

Devon drove. We got there and met with John King and Joan Welch. We set up the conference room and at 11:00 am the nine members of the MWAA committee trooped in. Devon was so wound up that he launched before the Committee members were able to introduce themselves. They stopped him so that they could, and then Devon relaunched.

Despite his level of excitement he was excellent. Then John King spoke on behalf of Provident. He was a pro. He couldn't have been any better. All four of us answered questions. I couldn't have asked for more.

Devon drove us back to Georgetown, and brought me up to date on his impression of Provident.

This was his take:

"The proposal was a 50-page document filled with graphs, maps and prose extolling the virtues of Southern Financial and telling the Airport Authority how wonderful it would be for them if they picked us. I had a tremendous amount of help from Dianne Smith, who made the final documents into beautiful pieces of artwork. I hand-delivered the proposals — eight copies were required — to the office at the airport, as I did not trust even Federal Express to get these precious documents to their destination. A couple of weeks later I got a response from the management of the airports asking for clarification on several points of the proposal. I sent the new documents as quickly as I could, and lo and behold, the airport management asked me to come and do a presentation to them in person. Excited beyond belief I began to prepare for the presentation. Two days into these preparations, I received the news that Southern Financial was being sold to Provident.

Some people thought I had known about the sale but I never had even a hint. I had mixed emotions about the sale, as did most of Southern Fincancial's employees, but I resolved to continue with the airport proposal. At Rod's suggestion, I brought in some Provident people to assist me, most notably, John King, the head of Provident's retail operation. John King seemed to me to be a stand-up guy with a good head on his shoulders. John King's contributions to the proposal were quite helpful, too, but as I worked with Provident I began to see some disturbing trends emerge. The first issue that caught my eye was some serious problems with the marketing department. I noticed there were 50-odd people in the marketing department, and they outsourced everything. I decided that I needed a brief history of Provident for the revised final proposal, and I called Lillian Kilroy to ask for a one- or two-page document delineating the admittedly fascinating 125-year history of Provident. Most companies keep such a document in their files that can be readily produced for presentations and marketing purposes. It took Provident three days to produce the document. I briefly looked over it and much to my chagrin I realized it was filled with grammatical and spelling errors. In all honesty, it looked like it had been written by an 8th grader — and not a very smart one at that."

Rod: Georgia and I talked all weekend. What we learned from our feedback from Diane, Cristen, Devon, Jacques and all the loan officers confirmed the picture that had been building in our minds. We were right. Provident was a wonderful retail bank. If the tables were turned, and if we were buying them instead of them buying us, we'd put John King in charge of our retail operation in a second.

However, they were a lot like a Japanese bank.

- They were very hierarchical. Their Group Managers had privileges such as luxury cars, which none of their subordinates could aspire to.
- Their staff departments were all-powerful and over-staffed.
- Their line people had no power.
- And very importantly, they had absolutely no women in important line jobs.
- Their HR department was all-important and talked in jargon. One of their critical people in HR worked only on retention. Lifetime employment! If they fired or demoted a department head, that person received six months' severance. That was job security. (This was to prove a major problem for them in the Southern Financial merger. Our people didn't like to be demoted.)
- And they traveled in packs. They had 18 people in our Middleburg branch looking at our facilities. Our staff complement in Middleburg was four FTE's. I'm starting to talk like them. That means full-time equivalents.

The Post Game

In a mass-market retail business you don't want any entrepreneurs. Staff departments find out what works and then keep everyone on script. You give everyone goals and measure them; you figure out what it means. Creativity and innovation are things that are anathema, on the line, to mass-market retail banking.

Provident had incredibly detailed job descriptions that were totally in jargon. They would be comical if it weren't so sad. As Tom Baker was fond of saying: "I can't make this up!"

The Japanese banks were all excellent retail banks, but at that time they were all bankrupt or on the brink because they couldn't handle business lending. The entire country had been a mess since 1989 for the same reason. The Japanese banks always had lifetime employment, except for women who were supposed to leave and get married in their late 20s.

At Southern Financial the legend was, if you were able to get up the stairs next to Georgia's office in the morning, because she was always one of the first people in and she believed she should fire you in the morning, you were OK for another day.

In the early years we had to be brutal. There were lots of people that didn't make the grade. We told you the Mr. Beasley story. But he wasn't alone. There were a lot of others who didn't make the cut.

And not only loan officers. Around the time of the merger there was not a single technology person in place from when I came on board in 1998. In several jobs we'd gone through three incumbents.

On Monday, December 8th we went to work in Georgetown then drove to Baltimore for lunch with Gary and Kevin. We talked for about 15 minutes about our new house in Italy.

Georgia: *Rod told them that they were like a Japanese bank. It didn't seem to have much of an impact since Gary asked whether that was good or bad. Rod said good for a retail bank, but very, very bad for a business-oriented bank. Virtually all of* *the Japanese commercial banks were bankrupt. Either they didn't care or it went over their heads. Rod could have been speaking Japanese.*

Rod: I also told them my Ed Yeo story from my Morgan Stanley days. Since I haven't told you this story I'll tell it here. (**Georgia:** *I normally hate Rod's stories but this one is important!*)

After I joined Morgan Stanley my boss was the inimitable Ed Yeo. Among other things Ed was Under Secretary of the Treasury during the Nixon administration. He is a book unto himself, but I won't start it here. I ran money market trading and sales, medium term notes and commercial paper. I had a lot fewer direct reports than I had at Chemical. But Ed and other Morgan Stanley partners managed to convince me that what I was going to do was going to be a lot more important than what I'd done at Chemical. I drank the Kool Aid.

What *was* true was that when Morgan Stanley was still really Morgan Stanley — before Dean Witter bought them — it was an extraordinarily talented, driven group of people, who could have done anything. I remember Ed Yeo saying at our third recruiting breakfast in one of the Morgan Stanley dining rooms, smoking our breakfast cigars, that if there were a financial disaster, the Morgan Stanley partners would get together in the ashes and start over. Powerful stuff.

After a couple of weeks in my new job I was seized with the need to have some structure in my new department. I sketched out an organization chart, just as I would have done at Chemical, and sat down with Ed. As I pulled it out Ed said in his sonorous voice, "Rod, put that away. We'll pretend we never saw it. We don't do that at Morgan Stanley."

It took me a long time to understand it, but I ultimately did: at Morgan Stanley the rainmakers weren't managers. No one even pretended they were. The rainmakers did their thing and had exalted seniority and titles and got paid commensurately. The managers and highly skilled technicians also did their things and got paid as well. When there was a task to be done a team would coalesce around it like a blood clot without reference to any hierarchy or organizational chart. It was a process to which the existence of any organization chart would have been inimical. It was the diametric opposite of the way

Provident Bank functioned. Gary and Kevin listened politely to the story and had no comment.

Georgia: *It was after Rod told this story that I realized they weren't listening and didn't intend to. That was fine with me. I just wanted to close on the deal as soon as possible.*

THE LAST CHRISTMAS PARTY

Rod: On December 13th we had our 18th and final Southern Financial Bank Christmas Party. Like the first 17 it was at our house, at Marblehead Farm in The Plains, where the bank had begun its life. That year we had 325 invitation acceptances — more than ever before. Tents wrapped the house on two sides.

Georgia and I didn't do any of the event setup. Julia Woodson would normally have decorated the house, but she was still ill. Shanna, Bertie Loos and Laura Vergot did everything and it was magnificent. There was a beautiful tree with gold ornaments and poinsettias everywhere. The house was incredibly festive and warm and Devon laid fires in all three fireplaces. Shanna destroyed her nails cleaning everything. A full bar and two bartenders probably contributed to the success of the party.

People make the party and this one was incredible. Georgia and I had expected our people to be depressed and apprehensive, but it was the absolute opposite. Georgia and I talked separately to Donna Richards, Jacques Smith, Ben, Gaye Boyette, Diane Smith and others with their spouses. All of them had been totally crushed 30 days ago. All of them were in fight mode tonight. They knew how good they were after talking to their counterparts at Provident. To a man, and to a woman, they were prepared to fight inside Provident or go outside to new opportunities. Donna said we should start another bank, which we could have. We didn't have a non-compete.

Georgia: *We didn't have Andre Fox, whom we'd had in attendance for years, because he'd been booked very early. But we did have karaoke, which we'd had for five or six years.*

I gave some brief remarks and then said, "Linda, Laura and I are going to sing Southern Financal's Anthem, 'My Way.'" And we did, with enthusiasm, with feeling, with gestures that would have put Loretta Lynn to shame, but largely without melody. Still, we truly believed we were absolutely great.

Rod: We danced like crazy. Carey brought out "her girls" and danced with Devon. Van fell in love with Linda. When she pushed him, he admitted it was because she was rich.

At the end the DJ called us up, at Linda's behest, to sing Jimmy Buffet's great classic "Let's Get Drunk and Screw." Devon, Linda, Bill Stevens and I all sang enthusiastically. Our melody was better than Georgia, Linda and Laura's, but their gestures were better. After we finished I told everyone that they shouldn't tell Provident we sang that song because we'd flunk our "civil training." (I don't understand for the life of me why they don't call it "civility training," but I'm not going to go to find out why.)

CHAPTER SIX
POST GAME ANALYSIS

Post Game Analysis

Rod: Let us say this upfront: we did not and do not want to run Provident either separately or together. "If nominated we will not run. If elected we will not serve."

We're in an extraordinary position. When this deal closes on April 30, 2004, we'll be the largest individual shareholders of PBKS (Provident Bank's NASDAQ ticker symbol) and we'll have enough money to do whatever we will want to do. There will be a couple of institutional shareholders who will be larger, but we'll clearly be important.

There's not a lot of precedent. Normally, shareholders in our position would serve gratefully and quietly. But that's just not possible anymore, certainly for us. We understand the business. We're the only shareholders other than Peter Martin who have any understanding at all of the business. More importantly, since Sarbanes Oxley was passed, it's very risky to serve on the Board of a company where management has no interest whatsoever in listening to your ideas. As Kevin said, "You may have a better mousetrap. But we bought you. Bad things happen in mergers." His was a self-fulfilling prophecy.

Things deteriorated quickly. Georgia had a call from Gary, who told her what the proposed organization structure for the commercial lending group was going to be. Linda Sandridge, who was Southern Financial's head of Commercial Lending, was to report to Tom Grantham, who is an absolutely wonderful guy, but who had much less seniority. Linda and her assistant had a portfolio of over $200 million and Tom and his group had a portfolio of significantly less. We love Tom, but what they were trying to do was simply to humiliate Linda. Tom is one of the world's best real estate lenders, but he has little interest in straight C&I loans.

We said no and set a meeting where we were at our most conciliatory. They were obdurate. Afterward we drove back to Washington. Late that afternoon there had been a truck accident that closed I-95 going south. We detoured onto another route, but it still took us four hours. Georgia cried most of the way home.

Georgia: *After our meeting we began to suspect that the problem was resentment from some of the senior people at Provident at how well Linda had done at Southern. The stock Linda owned and her options were ultimately worth well over a million dollars. Linda had been cocky from the beginning. She told us right after the merger was announced that she didn't have to work anymore, and that she would retire. She said that I'd been her boss for 17 years and that she didn't need to break in a new boss now. I convinced her that she should stay with Provident and work at least several more years. That's why I was devastated when they decided to humiliate her.*

I don't think Linda ever knew how hard we fought for her. Over the next several days we negotiated a good settlement for Linda with a great attorney from Bracewell Patterson. In the middle of everything Linda's mother was diagnosed with stage three ovarian cancer and was admitted to the University of Virginia Medical Center in Charlottesville, Virginia.

Rod: We began to have problems with our good customers. One of our best customers was a company called Halifax Corp. It was a public company, one of the very few public companies that did business with Southern Financial. We'd helped them through some problems. They'd had a fraud case that cost them a lot of money before they came to bank with us. The two principals, Chuck McKnew and Joe Sciacca, were immensely proud of what they'd done — and justifiably so. In late 2003 Georgia and I and Marie Taylor Leibson, the Southern account officer for Halifax, had lunch with Chuck and Joe at the Bistro Francais in Georgetown. They told us about two immense new contracts that they expected to be awarded, which would necessitate an increase in their ARTS line. We spent an hour with them going through the details and everything sounded fine. They were on the cusp of becoming a seriously important company. We told them the increase in the ARTS line would have to be submitted to Provident, but also that we didn't expect a problem. The line increase was to be subject to their being awarded the contract. After the lunch Marie submitted the request for the increase to Provident.

Three weeks later somebody at Provident decided they needed to meet with Halifax before they could approve any increase. Initially they wanted a junior credit person to meet with Chuck and Joe. Georgia said no. She and I would meet with them along with Marie and Kevin Byrnes, Provident's President, and Les Patrick, Provident's Senior Credit Officer. That would have been appropriate because if Provident approved the increase it would have been Provident's largest non-real estate C&I loan.

Gary called Georgia and for reasons we've never understood was inflexibly insistent that Les Patrick could not be at the meeting. It would be Kevin and Hugh Newton, their Group Head for Commercial Lending.

The meeting took place in our Georgetown office conference room on February 2, 2004. It was cordial enough with Kevin trying to exude goodwill and talk about how strong Provident was in retail business, particularly home equity lines. (That was all true, but if your audience doesn't care, forget your programmed script.) Finally Joe Sciacca, the CFO, asked when Provident was going to address their request for an increase in their line if they got their new contracts. Kevin tried to answer but fumbled, finally admitting that he didn't have any idea. That's the wrong answer when you're talking to a successful businessman for whom the company is his life.

After the meeting was over everyone stood around Kevin, who tried to reassure Chuck McKnew, the CEO of Halifax, that the credit approval process wasn't going to change. "We have a committee, but we're all just rubber stamps for Les Patrick," Kevin said. The problem was that Les Patrick was nowhere to be seen. We never gave them everything they wanted, but Chuck and Joe knew when he talked to us that we were two-thirds of the credit approval process — and for better or worse could make a decision.

I told Georgia that Chuck was trying, but Joe Sciacca's body language was totally negative.

The next day we took Amtrak to Newark Airport to connect with an Alitalia flight to Italy. We were to visit Florence and Rome to buy some furniture for our new place in Tropea. But with phones and Blackberries you're never really away unless you willfully cut yourself off.

We had immediate crises on the train. The first was Halifax. Marie emailed us that she'd talked to Joe Sciacca that morning and he'd asked, "What was all that about?" He went on to say that he had a term sheet from BB&T offering more than they had requested from us, and if Provident didn't answer them by the close of business today they were gone — even though he liked ARTS better than anything BB&T had to offer. Georgia called Gary and put it squarely in Provident's lap.

The second crisis related to Diane Smith, our Head of Marketing. She had been our branch manager in Fredericksburg and responded to my posting of the marketing job in 1999. She came up for an interview and I was skeptical. She didn't have a college degree and her only experience had been with Union Bank in Bowling Green. Warrenton is not the center of the world creatively, but Bowling Green is worse. (Apologies, Diane!) But she wanted it so badly she was willing to drive three-and-a-half hours a day from her home in Caroline County to Warrenton. And this was after she'd had her son.

Diane turned out to be superb. She took courses in everything and got better every year as we grew and the demands on her increased. She was the antithesis of the Provident mono-tasking model and she threatened Lillian Kilroy, Provident's powerful Head of Marketing, from the first night.

It never occurred to me until the Provident deal that the Head of Marketing could be "powerful." Marketing people are supposed to be creative professionals. They are measured by the quality of their work product. If they outsource everything they have no work product to measure. If someone criticizes their work product they simply fire the agency which produced it. Their existence becomes a game to see how much control they can exert over other departments. Maintaining unmerited power becomes an end to itself and is like a cancer within an organization.

While we were in Italy I had a very bitter email exchange on my Blackberry with Kevin Byrnes. I couldn't conceive of Provident not wanting to retain a talent like Diane, who could have saved them a bundle of money by internally doing a lot of the things Provident outsourced. I vastly underestimated the power of a threatened bureaucracy and Kevin basically didn't care.

Georgia: *We got back from Italy on February 16th and were immediately drawn back into the people problems inherent in the integration. They told everyone at Southern Financial what their job — or lack thereof — with Provident would be by the end of February. The Human Resources Department arrived in force in various locations and sat down first with the people who would* not *be offered jobs. Jeanne Uphouse, Head of HR, personally conducted many of the interviews. We soon learned two interesting things that were to become problems over the next two months.*

First, under Provident policy, any department head who was terminated or demoted was entitled to receive six months' salary as severance. Non-department heads received a week per year of service.

Second, Jeanne Uphouse was committing our pay for stay fund to the people who were to be terminated without ever consulting us. That was in total contravention of the definitive agreement. I was furious, but they didn't think it was a big deal.

Rod: On the 29th of February, a Sunday, we had lunch at Aditi's, an Indian restaurant in Georgetown. Aditi's is owned by Suku Nair, an outstanding local businessman, and a very long-time customer of Southern Financial. After lunch I suggested that Georgia call Linda in Charlottesville, where her mother was in the hospital.

Georgia: *I reached Linda in her room at the Omni Hotel and we talked for half an hour. She's knew her mother was not going to make it, but she was still, understandably, distraught. Her mother lived with her and was her best friend. She'd deteriorated very rapidly.*

Right after I hung up Rod and I talked and he suggested that we drive down to Charlottesville and take her out for dinner. I agreed and called her back. Someone else answered my call. I said, "I want to speak to Linda Sandridge." A woman said that she was from the University of Virginia Emergency Services squad. She said Linda had had a seizure, was on oxygen and was on her way to the UVA emergency room.

Rod and I immediately threw our clothes into a suitcase and got into the Range Rover for the drive to Charlottesville. On the way down we made a reservation at the Omni.

About three hours later we walked into the ER. We went up to the desk to ask for Linda and were intercepted by Rick Dixon, an old friend of Linda's who lives an hour's drive south of Warrenton. He said immediately, "She has a brain tumor." I said immediately, "I know her mother is very sick. How is Linda?" "You don't understand, Linda *has a brain tumor!*"

It was a kick in the stomach. We went up to Linda's room and she was conscious, in good spirits and already dealing with the fact that she was going to have surgery. Still upset about her mother who was on a different floor, Linda was already making jokes. "I'll never say again that 'this isn't brain surgery!'"

The next day we visited her again and were there when her brain surgeon and his interns came to talk to her. Dr. Jane was very impressive and didn't shy away from saying he was probably the best brain surgeon in the country.

Linda had her surgery about 10 days later and recovered completely. Linda's mother died about two weeks later.

The HR Interviews

Georgia: *After the interviews with the people who were not being offered jobs, HR Department staffers sat down with the people who were going to be offered jobs. After those interviews the Southern Financial people were supposed to sign a statement that they accepted the job and the terms and conditions connected with it.*

It was an absolutely unmitigated disaster. There was a virtual firestorm among our people. We called Gary Geisel and told him he was going to lose the commercial lenders unless he did something. He was concerned enough to come down on March 3rd to get our input.

Rod: Before Gary arrived I summarized the essence of what the HR people had told the Southern Financial people — or at least what our people had heard — on one sheet of paper:

- You're not going to get any options in February '04.
- You're not going to have a salary review in July '04.
- You'll no longer receive a car allowance. You'll fill out the forms and receive 36 cents a mile.
- We won't credit your service with Southern Financial to our pension plan.
- To Michelle Douglas: We don't know where your office will be.
- To Mary Ellen Clancy: We don't know whether your accumulated sick leave will carry over.
- You may receive bonuses, but they generally won't be what you're used to and they are only once a year. (Lillian to Diane Smith: "And they probably won't trickle down to your level.")
- In December '04 we'll tell you what your title, job grade and salary will be going forward. (Hugh Newton to Marie Taylor Leibson: "You'll have to trust us.")

When our meeting was over Gary asked for a copy and I gave it to him.

Another problem was that none of the line managers participated in the interviews. In other words, if there was bad news it wasn't coming from your future boss. It was coming from a bureaucrat.

Devon had been gung-ho about the prospect of joining Provident. At his interview, however, he heard for the first time that he was losing most of the department he'd built from scratch. His future boss had never mentioned it in their previous meetings. Only two of his 10 direct reports would continue to report to him. The Merchant Services business, which Provident didn't do and really didn't like, would be transferred to another department at Provident. Devon decided to leave completely on his own and take the severance.

Georgia: Marie Taylor Leibson was the account officer for Halifax and many other good customers. She had joined Southern Financial nearly 10 years earlier. She was a CPA, but until she joined us had never been a lender. We had dropped her in the water and she swam. She was one of our top producers in Northern Virginia. Equally importantly she had developed deep and broad relationships with the Small Business Administration (SBA), both in Richmond and in the Washington, DC regional offices. She received an incredible offer from another bank about five years before the merger and the Board had approved a substantial options package to keep her.

The Provident people had met her and wanted to keep her. They weren't stupid. If an institution wanted to be an important factor in small- and middle-market business in Virginia, north of Richmond to Washington DC, it would have to have Marie. Initially she was enthusiastic about Provident. Rich Hunt, who had just joined Provident, put on a full court press. I took her temperature from time to time and she seemed to be fine.

After her HR interview she left me a message to call her back. She said, "Georgia, you asked me to tell you if I couldn't work here anymore. Well, I can't and I'm leaving." I asked if there was any way I could change her mind. She said, "They just don't get it. In my HR interview I started out talking about a subordinate. I wanted to know what would happen if my subordinate had stupendous performance, off the charts for her salary grade and job classification. I guess I was really talking about myself. The HR staffer said, 'We don't pay the person, we pay the position.' I was out of there." She added that Hugh Newton had the nerve to call her at home and tell her she had to trust Provident. She told him that trust is earned and that neither he nor Provident had earned it. Marie then said to me, "I always knew where I stood with you. I often didn't agree, but it was always clear where you were coming from."

I wished her well. Since she was going to a competitor I told her I would accept two weeks' notice. Ultimately, another loan officer and most of the loan closing department followed her to the other bank.

A couple of days later Mary Ellen Clancy, the Head of Southern Financial's loan closing department, told me that she had sent back her Provident form as required.

POST GAME ANALYSIS

I assumed she had accepted and was staying. But then she said that Rick Steele was pressuring her to tell him how she had responded. That was my first inkling that she wasn't going to accept the Provident offer. She then admitted that she thought her new job was a demotion. Only loans under $100,000 were to be closed in Warrenton. She told Provident that she wasn't going to accept the position and asked for severance. I asked her what she was going to do and she said she had no idea, but felt good about it. She added that when she had learned that Devon was leaving she thought, "I knew this was a place where I didn't want to work."

About a week later she told me Provident turned down her request for severance because, according to them, she hadn't been demoted. She'd already written her response, which she read to me. It sounded fine. There was no way her new job wasn't a demotion.

After another couple of days she called me again and said they'd said no to the severance request again.

Mary Ellen wouldn't admit it, but she was over 50 and had worked for the bank for more than 10 years. The fact that she'd had a tummy tuck should have been irrelevant. (I love to tease her about that!) She should have gotten the same benefits that Devon received and others would get.

I told her we'd work on it. We checked with Bracewell Patterson and wrote a request under the terms of the definitive agreement to pay her part of the $300,000 "pay for stay" fund to remain in place until the closing. If there was anyone I needed until then it was Mary Ellen. Gary responded, "permission denied." I was aghast.

Furious, I called him and told him he was nuts. He would have a lawsuit on his hands for discriminating against a woman over 50 with 10 years of service with the Bank. He responded that he hadn't understood it was severance. They had decided that the largest "pay for stay" payment would be $15,000. That had to be from some ad hoc committee. (Remember, that wasn't their decision to make. They didn't give a shit about our legal agreement.)

He said he'd get back to me and ultimately did. They finally did the right thing, but put us through hell to get it done. (We never understood why. The bureaucracy?)

Rod: Consciously and unconsciously we wanted the last month to be our valedictory. We wanted to go out with style and most importantly to connect with a lot of people who were our friends.

The last Fairfax Advisory Board was on March 31st at Shanker Patel's Best Western in Fairfax City where we'd had so many events over the years. We had a full turnout thanks probably to Sam Belk. Georgia covered the fourth quarter of 2003 and the year as a whole. I talked about the Essex Bancorp closing, which had taken place at the end of February. Devon made a presentation about the Product Scorecard, which he did at the end of every quarter. His department had super results. We handed out the last Annual Report and told everyone how Diane had done it all, except for the picture of herself and Cristen.

We introduced Kevin Byrnes, who had agreed to talk for five to 10 minutes and introduce Provident. He had a slide presentation, but he couldn't get his slides to work. (He couldn't get himself arrested!) He went on for 35 minutes describing at times the slides he would have had if they had worked. He talked about how good Provident is in the retail business, which it is. He discussed the Portuguese sailor who started the bank 125 years earlier, about their new advertising campaign at Orioles games, about how they train their people in the supermarkets and how they started "totally free checking" in 1993. (He again neglected to say that Southern Financial had offered it beginning in 1986.) He grated once again, but we behaved and didn't say anything. Devon told us later that he'd left the meeting feeling sick to his stomach.

The next morning we worked in Georgetown until just after lunch and drove down to Richmond in the rain on I-95. We got to the West Broad branch just after 3:00 pm and kibbutzed with Joe Kellum and Marc. Hugh Newton, from Provident, arrived and I took him aside. I told him that Kevin's presentation the night before had been rude. He was our guest and he'd been obnoxious. I told Hugh that if he spoke for more than 10 minutes we'd remove him with a hook or worse.

After I spoke to Hugh we went across the street to get set up. The Richmond meeting went better than the one in Fairfax. Hugh kept it to 10 minutes and was a lot classier than Kevin had been, and I told him so after he spoke. I also told him that I just didn't understand why he and Kevin persisted in doing things that made Georgia and me absolutely furious, when their actions had no clear objective. I said that we were going to be on Provident's Board and would be their largest non-institutional shareholders. He made a face when I mentioned Kevin, and shrugged.

On Saturday, April 17th, we had the 18th and final Southern Financial party at the Middleburg Spring Races. The sky was clear when we got up and the ambient temperature shown in the Range Rover was 72 degrees when we left Georgetown to drive to Middleburg. Glenwood Park is a couple of miles north of Middleburg. It is an absolute gem. A local family lets it be used several times a year for horse races to benefit local charities. Eighteen years ago we had a tailgate party on the rail short of the finish line for five people in our jeep. Over the course of the past 18 years it's become a much more serious party. We've moved to the best location on the course, on top of the hill right up from the finish line. In April 2004 we had 125 acceptances from longtime customers and friends — many one and the same.

I've worried that it would seem frivolous to tell you about a party, even though it's been going on for 18 years, but it's not frivolous. This party is at the center of the fabric of what our Bank was: relationships with individuals and families.

Relationships are difficult and emotional, particularly when you're lending someone money. If you've ever lent a family member money you know what we're talking about. For the people who came to our annual party it was a relationship that in many cases had been tried and had triumphed. These were people with whom we often shared the same foxhole. Some of them were our heroes. Some of them needed help. But all of them were part of the fabric of our lives.

Our objective at the final Spring Races gathering was an ambitious one and probably totally unrealistic. We wanted to transfer these complex relationships to Gary and Kevin. Georgia and I carried them on our shoulders for years.

When we got there at about 11:00 am Diane Smith and Shanna Coffey were working on putting up the decorations alongside the small army of caterers who were setting up the tables. Muhammad Esfahani, a very long-time customer in Georgetown, was also there. He said that he was early, but that he'd like to help. He took off his jacket and helped Dianne and Shanna hang pictures.

Customers started to arrive. Who they were tells you a lot about the Bank, and a lot about the fabric of our lives. In addition to Muhammad, there were Len and Dale Adler, long-time customers of Southern Financial. Len was a heavy-duty real estate developer and investor in Northern Virginia. He was also a Director of Virginia Commerce Bank, a Northern Virginia competitor. Len and Dale were sailors, horse people and close friends — and fun.

There was John and Chris Milliken and their son Alex. John and Chris had been customers almost from the beginning. John was my campaign manager when I ran for the Presidency of the International School in the Hague, Netherlands in my senior year. I lost and have never touched politics at any level again. John stayed in politics, but worse, became a Democrat. He had an impeccable resume as a Virginia Democrat in important positions. I adore him, but won't use this book to advance his career. Sorry John.

Jim Williams, the owner of CIS, which provides security for large commercial ventures such as stadiums, and a longtime Southern Financial client, was also there. Also in attendance: Terry Kreamer, the CFO of ITA, one of our most exciting — and successful — technology clients. Terry never missed our party at the races. There was Pierre and Brigitte Lupesco, proprietors of ELSE, a fashion store in Georgetown, and who became our new partners after the sale to Provident. Bobby Mitchell, a Redskins Hall of Famer and super nice guy, along with his classy wife Gwen were there. They were close friends and Bobby was a shareholder and an Advisory Board Member, too. Ed Shields, Head of United Leasing near Richmond, and his former wife were there. Ed is an absolute prince of a guy and the last real gentleman in Richmond. We also welcomed Mitch and Clara Chambliss, long-time customers of the Bank and our travel agents for years.

We also saw Peter Jarrowey and his daughter. Peter had a variety of commercial interests including a golf course and a quarry that were all clients of Southern Financial. Even Peter would admit that he was a high-maintenance client, but he was a charming guy. Linda told him that he was the cause of her brain tumor.

Also: the Reuter family, including Dr. Nancy and DeeDee Reuter, the architect who designed the addition to our house in the Plains — and if she'd let us be her agent would have been the next Frank Lloyd Wright — as well as Jock and Debby Reuter, successful realtors in Middleburg. The Reuter family had been in Middleburg and Aldie since the early 1700s, and our friends for 20 years to that point. Several of their ventures were Southern Financial clients.

There was Dr. Hurt, a major client who owned about a third of Charlottesville and his wife, Alicia, a charming woman from Argentina, as well as Peter Colasante, who owns the Galerie L'Enfant in Georgetown, and his partner Anne, an excellent painter whose atelier was at that time in Puerto Rico. Peter also brought John Cord, another painter who lived in a mansion in the Azores for eight months a year and in an apartment in Shockoe Slip in Richmond for another four.

John and Joan Belotti were there, too. John was an extraordinarily successful Fairfax County businessman, and was one of our Directors. Joan was a successful horse breeder in Fauquier County — and much more charming than John. John's company was a client of the Bank's.

Gigi Winston the most charmingly flakiest and successful real estate agent in Washington DC and her family were there, as was Bruce Jennings, a successful businessman in Fairfax, who had been a Director of Horizon Bank before our merger. He'd also become a friend.

There were many others. It would be hard to assemble a more eclectic and interesting group of people. The day was beautiful and almost everyone was mellow. Mitch Chambliss sat down with us on the rail and thanked us for standing by them when they'd gotten in trouble several years earlier. He also thanked Devon for "mentoring" his son Robert. He said, "There will never be another Southern."

Richard Reed who'd been a good customer for years, and then sold his business to live a life of leisure, asked Georgia for a job. He didn't really need one.

Kevin Byrnes of Provident and his wife arrived around 2:00 pm. Gary Geisel and his wife arrived around 2:30 pm. We tried to introduce them to everyone but some key people had already left. Then they left by 4 pm.

Devon was organizing the betting, a simple pari-mutuel system, which he had done since he was 11 years old. By the time of the last Spring Races party he was 27. He had Peter Jarrowey's daughter, who was 11 years old, be his runner and his knee cracker. She was extremely good at it and has a clear career path at least until she's 17.

Dr. Metters, the CEO of Metters Industries, was the only guest who was uptight. Dr. Metters was a former General and holder of the Congressional Medal of Honor. He had a big new contract and needed an increase in his ARTS line to fund it. The requested increase had been pending with Provident for weeks. He called me several times the following Monday.

The party went on until 6 pm. It was weird. These were real people. These relationships were what Southern Financial had been all about. It was what Provident had actually purchased, but they didn't seem to care.

Georgia: *The weather was still beautiful on Monday, April 19th, 12 more days until the closing. It was actually hot. Rod and I went to our dentist to make sure that our teeth were in order before going away for four months. We both got x-rays and cleanings. It turned out we had to come back the next Monday. I needed a new cap and Rod a root canal.*

We got back to the office and I received a call from Bill Lagos. Provident still hadn't resolved his problem. Even worse, on Friday he had gotten a call from Dennis Starlipper, the CFO, who told him to stay for a couple of months and to trust them. Bill asked Dennis whether he'd read his contract. Dennis said no, and asked Bill what he wanted to do. Bill said he wanted to be paid out on April 30th and said that after that he would do whatever they wanted. Dennis said that would never happen and hung up on him.

Shortly after that Trish and Rick called Bill over to their office and suggested a side-letter guaranteeing that his estate get his payment if he died before June 30th, *which was what Bill wanted all along. But by that time it was too late. The trust that Dennis asked for had been eradicated totally.*

One more time they refused to do something that wouldn't have cost them any more than they were contractually obligated to do. The only conceivable explanation was that they wanted to keep a hammer on Bill for two months after closing. That was power. But it was also evil. Bill had devoted 15 years of his life to the Bank. He owned more stock than Kevin by a factor of 10. He had as much outright as Gary did. You figure it out.

They still hadn't come back to us on the charge-offs.

Our shareholder vote was in. Theirs was at 64% and needed 66 2/3% by Wednesday.

On Tuesday, April 20th, they were over the top on their shareholder vote. Their Annual Meeting was the next day. They released a weird press release on their earnings and on the proposed restructuring. The restructuring was going to cost them 22 cents a share in 2004 and another 6 cents in 2005, according to Henry Coffey at Ferris, Baker Watts. We were missing something and Henry was missing something. Why was that good? Part of the reason they made their earnings was a reduced loan loss provision.

Bill Lagos called me in the morning on Wednesday and said he'd made a decision. He didn't trust them and wanted to be paid out on the 30th. He would give up the pay for stay and the additional salary. Rod and I called Will Luedke and asked him to draft the documents which would pay Bill out on the 29th of April.

Just before noon, Robert Best, our partner at KPMG in Richmond, and Bill Stevens arrived. We were all to go through the 12 loans where Les Patrick wanted to take substantial charge-offs. Robert had been our Partner for nearly five years. Every quarter we'd gone through our reserve calculations with him. When we made acquisitions he made sure we didn't go overboard with our charge-offs. That afternoon he went through each loan with us and Bill Stevens to support what was the "right" number.

In the middle of the afternoon we called Billy and told him that we had set the process in motion to pay him out on the 29th and to pay his final salary and bonus payment the same day. We would probably have to fire him. He was emotional. For once no Billiverb. "You just shouldn't have to go out like this," he said. "I'll see you at the old timer's party on Friday."

At 5:30 pm Rod and I left with Robert Best and Bill Stevens having two or three loans still to go.

On Thursday Provident had its quarterly earnings conference call with the Bank analysts. It was wonderful that we didn't have to do that anymore. We called Trish and she thought it went fine."

Bill Lagos called in late morning and confirmed that he wanted to leave. He didn't want to take the risk that he would die sometime between April 30th and the date they wanted him to stay until. He'd made a lot of money on his stock, but he had kids in college and couldn't afford the risk. We called Will Luedke at Bracewell Patterson and asked that he set the legal documents in motion to do what Billy wanted to do.

Billy said to me, "If I'm this miserable you must be worse." He was right but it was one of those things you can't quantify.

Gary Geisel called me mid-afternoon about the charge-offs.

Rod: On Friday, April 23rd, we took the day off. The old timers party was at our house in Georgetown. We did our run along the river and ended up at Thai Kingdom on K Street. We couldn't stop talking about Provident. Georgia was furious. I was, too, but trying to understand what it was in their culture that made them the way they were. There was a pattern that was consistent from the first lunch with Gary and Kevin. They couldn't change once a staff department had issued an edict. They were totally dogmatic, right or wrong.

The old timers party was marvelous. We started out with cocktails and hors d'oeuvres. We gave all of the old timers a bound book containing the past five years of annual reports and the past five years of newsletters. They gave us a marvelous framed picture of the luxury cars everyone had bought with their options profits. It really summed everything up: American capitalism!

After cocktails we repaired to Café Milano, about four blocks down the street from our Georgetown house. It was pouring rain. Some took cars and the others walked.

We had a private room, which was necessary for what was to become a raucous group. Before the hilarity set in Georgia made a brief but great speech and gave all of the women rings with the Southern Financial logo and all of the men Southern Financial cufflinks.

Georgia: *When dinner started someone said to me, "Everyone looks so sad." I looked around the table at these wonderful people I'd worked with so long. Linda, who was having her first glass of wine since her brain surgery was simply ecstatic to be there at all and had a big smile on her face. Mary Ellen was animated and chatting away. Marie was expounding on something. Diane Smith was taking pictures with a digital camera and smiling from ear to ear. Devon and Shanna were off in a corner talking about something important. Only Bill Stevens and Michelle Douglas looked at all subdued. I said, "Look again. The people who are leaving look happy. Those who are staying don't."*

It was a telling moment. The people who had decided to leave had all made the decision to do something totally different, something scary but exciting. They were all apprehensive despite the fact that many had made a lot of money on their options. In Mary Ellen's words, "I feel good about my decision."

The leavers felt empowered. Some of the stayers didn't have a choice. They had no control over what was to come. They see an end to something they felt comfortable with, and knew they would miss working with people they enjoyed and trusted.

I felt good about everything. It was the beginning of a new phase in our lives and I was ready to take the plunge. It was easier for us since Rod and I had each other, profits from our stock options and a return of 10 times our original investment.

Bill Lagos came late and everyone applauded and cheered when he came in. He'd gone to play golf at his club and was tanned and relaxed. All of the "Billiverb" stories were retold. Billy roared. I saw Billy laugh so hard the tears streamed down his face. Trish, who'd been his boss for several years, had never heard many of the stories. The affection was palpable. Even Carmelita, who has fought with Bill for 15 years, decided she liked him.

Rod: Monday, April 26, 2004: I got in early. I called Gary and left him a long voicemail. He called me back mid-morning. He was Mr. Nice Guy. He said he was "optimistic" that they could get all the charge-offs they want.

They'd changed their minds about Bill Lagos. They really wanted him until June. "Then pay him out on Friday and re-hire him Monday," I said. Gary said, "We'd never do that; he has a double trigger on his contract." I noted they'd both been met.

I also told Gary that we'd been talking to Will Luedke at Bracewell and that we all agreed with our reading of Bill's contract. Gary said he would have Muldoon Murphy contact them, and hung up.

KPMG arrived shortly thereafter. They went through the loans again with Georgia, me and Bill Stevens.

At 12:00 pm Georgia and I had dental appointments that had been scheduled for two weeks, so we left the office. Georgia got a new crown and I had my first root canal. It was more fun than what was going on when we got back to the office. (I rate the root canal just under the colonoscopy.)

That afternoon we ended up concurring, based on Les Patrick's severe haircuts on collateral, on $4.5 million in charge-offs out of nearly $12 million proposed. One loan had clearly deteriorated. The others were all arguable. The next day we would take the charge-offs and close the books for the first quarter.

Georgia talked to Billy. Provident's controller was in Warrenton and panicked that he was leaving. She made another "trust us" entreaty. He declined and told his staff he was done. He told Georgia he was sick to his stomach and wanted out.

Later we talked with the KPMG partners about Les Patrick's contention that we'd been reporting our "past dues" incorrectly. He said that we had tens of millions of past dues that we hadn't reported. We told Les earlier that we'd been reporting them the same way for 18 years. How you report them is governed by the rules of how you report the call report to the Federal Reserve. Provident's KPMG Partner suggested we review the call report rules since we might have to restate our call reports and our 10ks. That would have been absolutely horrendous.

The following day we were in early again. I called Tim Armstrong, our Assistant Controller, and explained the problem. Tim has been doing our call reports for around 10 years and he did another bank's for years before that. He faxed me the regulations in minutes. We read it together and conclude that what we were doing was right and had always been. This was a simple canard, just as the overtime issue was.

They were doing it wrong. But the emotional stress was substantial. Do they know what they're doing? Are they doing it on purpose? Why do this now, three days from closing?

We passed the entries on the charge-offs.

Georgia and I had dinner at Café Milano, our home away from home, with Neil and Ellie Call, our friends of 25 years. Neil and Ellie were wonderful. Neil had been a Director of Southern Financial since before the beginning. We couldn't have been happier if we weren't so miserable.

Georgia: *Wednesday, April 28, 2004: Rod had to go back to Dr. Salwah to finish up on his root canal. He was a total baby.*

I got a call from Gary Geisel at about 10:30 am. Gary told me that we can't close Friday — or maybe ever. We were too far apart on the charge-offs. I said, "Gary, let's look at where we are," and we went loan by loan. He then said, "Do we replenish the reserve after the charge-offs?" I told him we never affected the reserve. He didn't have a clue. He said, "I don't know what I'm talking about. I'll call you back."

To fill out an absolutely surreal day, I got an email warning me that Lorenzo Bean III filed a complaint against Southern Financial Bank on behalf of a deceased client. Mr. Bean was John Chang's attorney in the Washington Bike case. He was seeking $750 in damages because of a CD held by his client, which reverted to a lower interest rate after it was not renewed, and $350,000 in punitive damages. The world had gone crazy.

We had to sign the closing documents that afternoon. The attorney from Muldoon Murphy (theirs) came to our office and was characteristically late. The Bracewell Patterson (ours) attorney as on time and cooled his heels in the lobby for 45 minutes. We signed everything and asked him about the closing Friday morning. He sent an email telling us the exact amount we will receive after withholding Friday morning. He said that it will be "first thing."

We don't hear anything from Gary until about 3:00 pm. He called and said he wanted to explain "the silence." He said he was waiting to hear from Terry Sweet, their KPMG partner, about several issues. They accepted our 1Q04 charge-offs and wanted to do more on Friday. They wanted as much cushion as they could have. I told him that he could do whatever he wanted as long as Terry Sweet approved it. He was comfortable with that and asked when Special Shareholders meeting would be the next day. I told him 3:00 pm. It was the last time heard from him until I called him on May 7th.

Rod: Thursday, April 29, 2004: Only two more days to go. We tied up a couple of loose ends and drove out to Warrenton. We met with Shanna and signed some account opening forms, moving our accounts to the Middleburg Bank. Then we drove out to the Fauquier Springs Country Club where we had our Annual Meetings for years. At 2:00 pm we held a brief Board Meeting. We told the Board everything that was going on, warts and all, as we always had. We passed the necessary resolutions and we gave all the women Southern Financial rings and all of the men Southern Financial cufflinks. We also gave them each a framed Board picture.

Georgia: Then we had the Special Shareholders Meeting, which was really a formality since the vote was already in. I made a speech about the people of the Bank and then Rod talked about the Board. Maybe it was just me but I felt an incredible warmth from the employees and shareholders.

Post Game Analysis

After the meeting we stood around for about an hour talking to employees and shareholders. No one wanted to leave. We finally led a caravan of Directors and spouses and SVP's and spouses to Marblehead Farm, where, miraculously, there was food and drink.

The party was excellent, one of our best. Tom Baker told and retold a story about trying to explain to Doug Durans of Provident, whom they call "Elvis," why the University of Virginia and Monticello are "historic." I think we had a culture clash. Laura Vergot was there with a mysterious "Colonel" and stayed until all hours. We loved her, but we finally suggested they go late in the evening.

The morning of Friday, April 30th, we still hadn't heard from Gary. That was supposed to be our very last day.

We drove into Georgetown from the farm. We talked to Bracewell Patterson en-route and learned that they had a "dry closing" with Muldoon Murphy the previous night. That was supposed to mean that they'd done everything they needed to do and everything should go smoothly. We authorized Bracewell to release the documents and proceed to closing just before 9:00 am. The payment of the cash portion of the deal for the large shareholders was still up in the air. They were supposed to send a "transmittal letter" the following Wednesday. Heaven knew when we and our shareholders would get our cash. But we hoped to get our one-time payments that day.

Rod: At 9:00 am Georgia began an Oneida Board Meeting via conference call and I was left to stand by the phones. By 10:00 am I was having chest pains — imaginary but compelling. At 10:30 am Georgia was off her call, and by 11:30 am two guys with Provident badges — they were big on badges over there — started scraping the Southern Financial Bank name off the windows and the hours of operation off the doors. They had no class. They hadn't closed and they hadn't paid us, and they were not going to wait to change the main signs until Memorial Day weekend a month later.

At 11:45 am we went downstairs for lunch. At noon we started calling Bracewell. Around 1:00 pm the Muldoon attorneys told Bracewell that the merger documents were filed and they were working on our wire. At 2:00 pm they said they were working on some problems with the documents and our wire. By 3:00 pm we were going crazy.

Then, at 3:15 Will Luedke and Charlotte Rasche called and told us they'd just talked with Kevin Byrnes and Bob Davis, who unilaterally decided to withhold $100,000 from each of Georgia's and my payments until they could recalculate the 280G payment limits. We'd already paid KPMG $40,000 in November and December to make those calculations. It was egregious that they waited until 3:10 pm on the very last day to tell us.

Georgia had two brief conversations with Kevin. She hung up on him and then he hung up on her. She called him a "sleazebag," but only because time pressure prevented her from finding a better word.

It was an awful end to what should have been a triumphant last day. Georgia was lower than whale shit and she should have been on top of the world. Telling her that she should be on top of the world didn't help at all. We both felt soiled and dirty.

***

On May 1, 2004, Southern Financial Bank was no more. Any institution made up of human beings is ephemeral — people with shared dreams and objectives. What we built was simply gone. We tried to take care of the people who were critical to our success. A lot of our people became very well off. Were we sad? Sure, but were going on to other exciting things. Linda, Shanna, Dianne and Devon were still with us. We bought a marina in the Northern Neck on April 21st. We bought half of a fashion store. We made a loan to Peter Colasante on 97 Impressionist paintings and we financed GRDM on buying 21 transitional housing units. All fun stuff. All things on which we think we're going to make money.

We got an email from Shanna on the 20th saying that our cash had arrived in our brokerage accounts, as it had for all the large holders. Provident couldn't bring themselves to do anything nice, even when it didn't cost them anything and it was going to be done anyway.

Post Game Analysis

The next day after the closing we took the Acela to New York where we stayed for just over two weeks in an apartment in SoHo that we shared with two of Georgia's brothers. The apartment was in a building that Georgia's grandfather bought nearly a hundred years earlier. It was the last asset of his estate. We had the ground floor apartment, which could have been wonderful if it were ever fixed up. We got a laminated map and crisscrossed all of Lower Manhattan, from Chinatown to the Meat Packing District, as shameless tourists. We tried every restaurant listed in Zagat's with a food rating over 22.

We spent time with family. My mother came for a long weekend and had an absolutely wonderful time, contrary to her expectations. We had some exploratory meetings with people we'd met in the Italian fashion industry. We proceeded as planned but Provident hovered.

On Tuesday the 4th they paid us most of the $200,000 they'd held back, but they kept $3,000 just so they would have something to discuss. In addition, part of the deal was that they were going to grant us 10,000 options on Provident stock immediately after the closing. It was in the definitive agreement and the S-4. But they didn't follow through.

On the afternoon of the 6th we got a frantic call from Devon. Bob Davis, Provident's Corporate Counsel, had just called Marc Harding, the M in GRDM, and ordered him to come to Baltimore on Thursday the 13th of May to be questioned about the Reynolds properties. Marc was sick. He had two children under 3 years old, had just bought a house and couldn't afford to lose his job. His only sin was that he was associated with Devon and us. He rationalized to Devon that he could probably find another job and go on unemployment in the interim.

It was absolutely the last straw for us. Everything we did was entirely above board. Jackie Fitterer had asked Marc a couple of months earlier to commission drive-by appraisals of the properties. He did and Jackie gave them to Provident. Provident in its wisdom decided to haircut them some more and told Jackie what to tell the attorney to bid. It was an open auction. Two of the properties went to other bidders. The rest went to GRDM with Devon bidding. Provident's response was to try to bully Marc. It was consistent, but we were not going to tolerate it anymore.

We talked a lot that afternoon and that evening. We had two alternatives, and we went back and forward between them for a month.

First, we could go on Provident's Board and try to fix the Bank. I leaned in that direction. I could see how to fix their marketing and their human resources departments. But it would be bloody and difficult. They hadn't seen fit to change Provident one iota or to keep any of the good things about Southern Financial. Why would they accept our advice once we were on the Board? Gary had absolutely no control over any of the staff departments. If Sarbanes Oxley weren't a paper tiger it is what we would do. It was Gary and Kevin's worst nightmare.

Georgia: *Our second choice of potential action was to never join Provident's Board at all. We could simply ride off into the sunset and enjoy what we'd earned. We'd be able to do anything we wanted. Gary, Kevin and Hugh would be ecstatic because they wouldn't have to change a thing and they wouldn't have to deal with us anymore.*

In the end, it wasn't hard to choose the second.

On the morning of May 7th I called Gary Geisel. I told Gary to lay off Marc. It was cruel. If they had questions about the Reynolds properties they should ask the two of us. I also told Gary that we did not intend to take the two Board seats they were obligated to offer us. The whole merger process had been too bitter for us to deal with him and the senior management in the future. We did, however, expect the remaining hold back and the stock options, which he assured me he would deliver.

On the 10th and the 11th we focused on trying to get our personal communications organized. We'd talked to Jacques Smith and Howard Hargrove months earlier about getting off the sofin email system before the closing. We'd bought a server, the domain name and the software to run our Blackberries on a private network. Our friend Howard was helping us. We'd ordered a DSL then a T1. By the 11th we were concerned. We were leaving for Italy on June 2nd and didn't have an email connection set up. I called the main number in Warrenton and asked them to page Jacques and Howard. I got Jacques, but it was a mistake. Five minutes later three Senior Vice Presidents were in front of Jacques and Howard asking what we wanted. That was sick. We obviously weren't hiding anything. There was something profoundly evil about Provident's culture.

Howard finally got us set up on our own server with a business DSL. We had a mini-network that drove our Blackberries, which, by then, Georgia could not live without. We bought two new T-Mobile phones in New York on the presumption that T-Mobile would work better in Europe. We were connected to the world, but after 18 years not through Southern Financial. It felt weird.

It wasn't until late on Friday the 21st that Provident issued a press release and an 8-K about the two of us not going on the Board. They said we'd informed them on the 18th. That wasn't true, but it was over. Finally.

Rod: They changed the signs beginning Friday the 28th, before the Memorial Day weekend when they did their conversion. It coincided with the peak of the locust hatch in Washington DC.

A few years later, on April 3, 2008, Nick Adams of Wellington Management called Georgia and left three phone numbers. He then called me and left the same three numbers. We got him just before 5:00 pm and all he wanted to talk about was Provident. He wanted to know what had happened to the SFB management team after the merger. He was interested in our perception of their underwriting. Georgia said that despite the mistakes they made on securities that her perception was that the loans were underwritten pretty conservatively. We were candid about our perception of the weaknesses in the senior management group — and the intrinsic value of their deposit franchise. We talked for about 45 minutes.

POST SCRIPT

Devon: That's the end of the Southern Financial part of their lives, but it's not the end of the story. Although Rod and Georgia enjoyed their time in Italy after selling Southern Financial, that proved to be short-lived. As they joked afterwards, they "flunked retirement."

Toward the end of 2004 they agreed to help start a boutique bank, but planned to have little daily responsibility other than being on the board and raising the initial capital. We're working on the sequel to this book, *Second Time Around: The Sonabank Story*. Stay tuned!

After their retirement, Rod and Georgia focused on what they loved: Rod bred and raced his Thoroughbreds, and they were never far from their beloved Springer Spaniels. Georgia and Rod helped her brother with the 501(c)3 Organization, The Michael G. Santangelo (MGS) Scholarship Fund. Both of them served on the Board of Directors and are one of the Foundation's major donors.

Merging their love for Marblehead Farm with their desire to help others, they not only provided a great education to underprivileged youth, but they also created new and exciting experiences for them. They built a dormitory at the farm to house up to a dozen students at a time, where they can ride horses, fish, and swim in the pool.

The MGS Scholarship Fund is growing by leaps and bounds. By the end of 2024 the foundation had raised a total of $600,000 with assets over $1 million. It put 35 students through a private high school education.

In June 2024, Rod passed away. We were all with him when it happened. Our hearts have been aching ever since. Georgia has leaned on her siblings, my wonderful cousin Kate and me, and some of her closest friends that she and Rod met along the way. She continues to be active with her investments, horses and the charity, and is doing as well as can be expected. She's tough as hell.

Those two had a love story like none other. For 44 years, through all the ups and downs, joy and stress and heartbreak, they were always a team first. Rod doted on Georgia so much. His face lit up when he bought her gifts for birthdays and holidays. He designed special jewelry items and would give them to her, beaming. She absolutely loved it. She did the same for him, getting him fancy fishing gear like fly rods, old books and horse stuff.

When Rod came to work at the bank they were finally able to be together 24 hours a day. I teased them, saying they would drive each other crazy. I mean, what couple do you know that wants to be together *that* much? But they were true soulmates. It wasn't a burden, it's what they had wanted all along. After that, they were never apart for more than half a day.

Post Game Analysis

They traveled extensively over the years, mainly to Europe and Asia, soaking in the cultures and foods of foreign cities. Sometimes they went back to a place several times. (There was an obsession with St. Bart's in the early 90s we don't talk about.) They walked and ran everywhere, in every city they went to. They found little hole-in the wall restaurants and raved about them, sometimes taking notes about where they went. They shopped for interesting antiques.

As time went by they gravitated more and more to Southern Italy, and through a bit of a fluke they found a charming village called Tropea. They bought a house and a guest house there that has given our family years of incredibly good times and memories.

Another thing that brought the two of them so close together was their shared joy in pursuing their hobbies. Through their travels over the years they built an eclectic antique collection to rival a small museum, and actually *built* a corkscrew museum, owned a marina for several years, and invested in a high-end clothing store. They dabbled in real estate and fashion. Rod built an amazing library.

For those of us who know them well, let's be honest, Georgia can have a bit of a temper. Rod, on the other hand, was a pretty mellow guy, so Georgia would have to poke him a few times to get him really riled up. But here's the thing: we all knew that Rod secretly *loved* it.

Another big part of their legacy is their "extended" family. Rod and Georgia really meant it when they said that their employees were like family. They didn't just make money for their investors, they raised up their people. There are Southern Financial and Sonabank alumni helping to run banks all over DC, Northern Virginia and Richmond. They created an entrepreneurial, conscientious culture that made for passionate employees and produced amazing results. That same spirit reverberates throughout community banking in our area to this day.

We dedicate this book, and the amazing story it tells, to Rod.

For all of the people reading this who worked for Rod and Georgia over the years, or did business with them, from Georgia and myself, we love you all.

***

Appendix A

10 Years of Success

Page 2

Appendix B

**Georgetown, Country Article -
Best Dressed (January 1999)**

Page 37

APPENDIX B CONTINUED

Georgetown, Country Article - Best Dressed (January 1999)

Page 37

APPENDIX C

Interest is compounded
Husband-and-wife team run Southern Financial

BY CAROL HAZARD, TIMES-DISPATCH STAFF WRITER
August 25, 2002

She's chairman and CEO. He's president and chief operating officer.

The married couple run Southern Financial Bancorp Inc., the sixth largest bank holding company in Virginia.

Southern Financial recently bought Metro County Bank, one of the first banks to open in this area after a run of large bank mergers in the mid-1990s and the first to be acquired.

"Our styles are so different," said Georgia S. Derrico, 57. "I'm a hot-tempered Italian."

"I'm a saintly WASP [white, Anglo-Saxon Protestant]," quipped R. Roderick Porter, 57.

"We've always had a volatile relationship," she said.

Married 21 years, they've been leading the business together, technically, for four years. But Porter has been on the board since Derrico started the Warrenton-based bank in 1986.

Twelve years into the business, Derrico still ran the show and approved all the loans. The Bank had grown to $250 million in assets and Derrico needed a No.2 person. She considered possible candidates and settled on one.

"I have an idea who I want to hire," she told her husband. "You."

If she thought her marriage could survive, she was advised to go for it, she said. Porter, a commercial and investment banker, knew nothing about retail banking.

However, the prospect of a "vastly improved commute" was tempting, he said, especially since he'd been catching an early shuttle flight to New York City every Monday and returning to Virginia Friday evenings every week for about 10 years.

His focus would be to help the company grow.

"If we left it all up to Rod, I don't know how big we would be," Derrico said.

In 1999, Porter commandeered the first acquisition, Horizon Bank of Virginia in Fairfax County. A year later, the bank added savings and loan offices in Springfield and Fredericksburg.

Another acquisition in 2000 was a bank technology company. "That set us apart," Porter said.

The purchase gave Southern Financial the ability to offer a cash management system to its primary customers - small- and medium-size businesses. Its customers could borrow and pay online without calling or stopping by the bank.

The addition of Metro-County Bank, with $96 million in assets and its five branches, gave the growing Southern Financial and $900 million in assets and 26 branches. It also was Southern Financial's segue into the Richmond market.

"We want to be in all the good, dynamic markets in the state," Porter said.

Southern Financial is a long way since its beginnings in a

R. Roderick Porter, president and chief operating officer of Warrenton-based Southern Financial Bank, and Georgia S. Derrico, the bank's chairman and chief executive officer.

garage on the farm that Derrico and Porter bought near Middleburg.

Derrico had been with Chemical Bank, now J.P. Morgan Chase, for 13 years when she left to start Southern Financial. "I wanted to do something entrepreneurial."

The only thing she knew how to do was start a bank. She raised about $4 million in capital, a feat, considering she knew no one in Virginia at the time and most of the directors had to be from Virginia.

Her hook was to ask people if they would like to be on her board. The main requirement was a $100,000 minimum investment.

The first branch opened in Herndon with three employees and three phone lines. The bank opened a new branch each of its first 13 years.

The bank was profitable in the second month of operation, Derrico said. Most new banks don't show a profit until the third year.

It's apparently still on a roll.

According to a Scott & Stringfellow report on the bank's second-quarter results, profitability was excellent and asset quality improved."

Second-quarter earnings rose 33 percent to 58 cents per share over the same period a year earlier, exceeding analysts' estimates of 51 cents per share, the report said.

In sum, we believe this was a superb quarter that exceeded our expectations on a number of fronts. Trends are favorable, and we believe management is doing an excellent job of growing its franchise in a profitable manner."

Reprinted with permission of the Richmond Times-Dispatch, Business Section

Richmond Times-Dispatch Article (August 2002)

Page 69

APPENDIX D

Reprinted from

AMERICAN BANKER
THE FINANCIAL SERVICES DAILY

Monday, September 10, 2001

Duo Has Expansion Plans for Va.'s Southern

BY JOHN REOSTI

Georgia S. Derrico and R. Roderick Porter, the husband-and-wife team that runs Southern Financial Bancorp Inc., admit to a mild case of what they termed "megalomania."

The $728 million-asset company is performing quite well in its little corner of northern Virginia, but the couple are determined to build Southern into a regional player from Richmond, Va., to the outskirts of Baltimore.

The Warrenton-based company took its first step toward that goal last month when it opened its 20th branch in the fashionable Georgetown section of Washington.

Later this year it plans to open an office in Charlottesville, Va., and next year it will set its sights on Richmond and Montgomery County, Md., the fast-growing Washington suburban county that is considered one of the best banking markets in the Middle Atlantic region.

To speed this phase of its expansion program, Southern is considering an acquisition or a branch purchase.

"If there's an opportunity to buy branches or a bank, we'll look at it," said Ms. Derrico, the chairman and chief executive officer. Southern is "striving to be a $1 billion-asset bank," she said.

Acquiring a banking company would hardly be out of character for Southern. It already has bought two: the $76 million-asset, Springfield-based First Savings Bank of Virginia in October 1999 and the $128 million-asset, Vienna-based Horizon Bank of Virginia last September.

Those purchases bolstered Southern's presence in Fairfax County, Virginia's most populous and wealthiest county.

Laurence C. Pettit, a senior vice president at Anderson & Strudwick Inc., a Richmond brokerage and investment banking firm, ranked Southern at the top of his list of potential acquirers. Southern's making a deal outside its core market is "probable," he said.

Buying mood? R. Roderick Porter and Georgia S. Derrico, the husband-and-wife team that runs Southern, say their plans may include another acquisition

William McKinnon, the president of McKinnon & Co., a Norfolk, Va., investment banking firm, added that Southern is "a regional bank, not a community bank."

"If they expanded further in the District of Columbia or moved into Maryland, it wouldn't surprise me at all," he said.

Mr. Pettit and Mr. McKinnon each said he expects Southern to achieve its goals, largely because of Mr. Porter and Ms. Derrico. Both got their starts in banking at Chemical Banking Corp. (now J.P. Morgan Chase & Co.), so "they have a different level of sophistication you don't see in most community banks," Mr. Pettit said.

Moreover, Southern has hired five other Chemical alumni as senior managers, most in the last three years, and Mr. Porter said that many of Southern's underwriting guidelines are "clones of Chemical's."

The model has worked well. As of Aug. 31, just 0.48% of Southern's $353.5 million loan portfolio was classified as nonperforming, and its loan-loss reserve was $5.5 million, or 1.57% of total loans.

"We like to keep our provision high," Mr. Porter said. "We've seen a lot of small banks get crippled because they couldn't afford to clean up their problem loans."

Ms. Derrico, 56, has headed Southern since founding it in a Herndon, Va., strip mall in 1986. (A self-described penny-pincher, she said she moved the headquarters to Warrenton in 1992 because the rents there were cheaper.)

Her husband was a founding member of the board of directors, but he did not take a management post until 1998, when he became the president and chief operating officer. He admitted that living and working together means they both "probably eat and drink the bank too much," but he said he enjoys the arrangement.

"My only rule is, no meetings before 7 a.m.," he said.

According to Ms. Derrico, though, their partnership is not entirely free of tension.

"I'm a count-the-pennies CEO," she said. "That's hard with Rod on board. He likes to spend money."

Southern has been generating plenty of profits lately. Its earnings last year rose 36.8% from a year earlier, to a record $5.2 million, and its $3.76 million of profits for the first half of this year put Southern on pace to better that mark. ∎

Reprinted by Thomson Financial • (800) 367-3989

Appendix E

MORE BANKING TECHNOLOGY FOR OUR COMMERCIAL CUSTOMERS!

In order to continue to provide our commercial customers with sophisticated services that until now have only been offered by larger impersonal banks, Southern Financial has formed our newest subsidiary, Southern WebTech.com.

Aidan Harland, President and CEO of Southern WebTech.com.

Upon receipt of Federal Reserve Bank approval, Southern Financial will buy the assets of the Darien Consulting Group which provides commercial banks with letters of credit and foreign payment and foreign collections systems. In the third quarter of 2000, we expect to offer those services on the web to our business customers.

Southern WebTech has begun the development of a state of the art Accounts Receivable Tracking System (ARTS) for small and medium sized businesses. The new system will combine a lockbox with unique accounting and tracking features. All collections will be directly deposited into your company's account the same day they are received by our Accounting Department. No more precious time wasted processing mail or going to the bank to deposit checks!

Southern WebTech's President and CEO, Aidan Harland, has relocated to Warrenton from Atlanta, Georgia. Originally from Yorkshire, England, Aidan attended Cambridge University and has been a U.S. citizen since 1963.

Aidan was President of the Darien Consulting Group since its inception in 1978. Prior to founding Darien, Aidan was Senior Vice President at American Express in charge of the North American Region and Corporate Relationships.

Before joining American Express, he spent seven years at Connecticut Bank and Trust Company where he was Senior Vice President, International and Corporate Division. He began his banking career at Chemical Bank where he was Vice President of Foreign Exchange and International Money Management (and Southern Financial President Rod Porter's first boss!).

Southern WebTech currently has contracts with eleven banks, including Allfirst, Harris, and Michigan National.

Southern Financial's customers will benefit greatly from Aidan's vast banking and computer experience!

More Banking Technology for our customers

Page 79

Appendix F

Georgia Derrico started the Southern Financial Bank as a savings and loan 12 years ago in Northern Virginia. The company now has 11 branches and is planning another here in Fredericksburg, scheduled to open this fall.

Breaking banking's barriers
Southern Financial CEO creates own niche in market

By TED BYRD
THE FREE LANCE-STAR

When Southern Financial Bank opens its first branch in Fredericksburg this fall, it will join a growing number of small banks here. One thing that will set it apart is its president, who will be the only woman running a local bank.

Georgia Derrico started the financial operation 12 years ago in Herndon. It now has 11 branches across Northern Virginia. If regulatory approval is given, the 12th will be a former First Virginia Bank building in front of Greenbriar Shopping Center on State Route 3.

Derrico spent 14 years with Chemical Bank in New York before taking off on her own.

"I decided I wanted to try something entrepreneurial," she recalled.

Her husband, a horse enthusiast, wanted to buy a farm in Middleburg. She thought northern Virginia would be a fine place to start a bank, so they moved south.

It took two years, but in April 1986 she had $4 million in capital to found the institution and open an office in Herndon.

Initially, Southern Financial was a federal savings and loan. It was converted to a state-chartered commercial bank in 1995.

In 1988 the company expanded to Middleburg, bringing the town its first automatic teller machine. Now there are branches in Winchester, Warrenton, Leesburg, Fairfax and Woodbridge.

Assets have grown as well. They increased 19 percent last year, to $227 million.

From the beginning, Derrico's strategy was to locate bank offices outside the Capital Beltway. And, after dealing with larger businesses at Chemical, she wanted to deal with small businesses in a more personal way.

"I'm going to emphasize plain-vanilla banking," is how she describes her thinking at the time.

After more than a decade, Derrico thinks the bank has come to understand the needs of small businesses.

"Sometimes, startups and small businesses need some handholding," she said. She personally visits clients with more than $200,000 in business with the bank.

Southern Financial also likes to provide customers all their banking services. If a customer has a business loan, the bank will seek to provide his checking account and home mortgage, Derrico said.

And while small banks need to personalize service, they also need to keep up with technological changes, mostly by contracting out to other companies who have the expertise, Derrico said. For example, her company is beginning to offer the option of home banking via computer.

It's not hard to spot small businesses that are likely to do well, she said. "If they have an idea or dream, you see pretty quickly if they've done their homework."

Southern Financial went public in 1996 and trades on the Nasdaq exchange.

The bank has projects in the Fredericksburg area, including financing for Shannon Airport, a roller hockey center and several restaurants, Derrico said.

She wants to build on that and hopes that the ongoing mergers of larger banks helps.

"Everyone says, 'When are you going to sell?'" she said. "I think we have a couple of years when we can really build our franchise. People want to be treated like a person, not a number."

'Breaking Barriers'

Page 89

APPENDIX G

Southern Financial Bank — *ahead of the rest!*

Volume 3, Number 4 — Fall 2001

Still On the Move

For several years, your Bank's closest investment banking relationship has been a company in New York called Sandler O'Neill. Herman Sandler, the head of the company, was an irrepressible, charismatic man who lived life to the hilt. More importantly he was a superb business strategist who was a wise counselor to the two of us. He was our friend. Jeff Smith was the research analyst who followed Southern Financial's stock. We went to NASCAR racing school in the Poconos with him last year. He had two small children. Christy Irvine was the market maker in Southern Financial's stock and she had just married. On September 11th, Herman, Jeff, Christy and sixty-seven of their colleagues died. We grieve for them.

Just last July we had visited Sandler's offices on the 104th floor of Tower 2 of the World Trade Center to plan for a secondary offering of Southern Financial's common stock. Herman took us out on his new motor yacht from the World Trade Center Marina to seal the deal.

We worked on the deal through August and were scheduled to file it with the SEC on September 11th. Jim O'Meara of Sandler O'Neill was at the printers that morning to put the finishing touches on the document. That saved his life. We decided to go ahead with the deal with Sandler O'Neill as sole manager out of respect for Herman and our other friends at Sandler. We filed on September 12th.

We completed the deal on October 17th. It's impossible to communicate what a roller coaster it's been. We spent several days in New York in Sandler's temporary offices but we can't begin to convey the emotion of the horrific stories we heard.

But what it comes down to is that we were "On the Move" before the attacks. We want Herman to know we're "Still on the Move." If we'd told that to Herman he'd have said something unprintable and then he would have laughed that marvelous friendly but mocking laugh that just welled up inside him. We will miss that laugh forever.

But we think he'd be proud.

Georgia Derrico and Rod Porter

Making A Difference

Jennifer Hall of SFB's Millwood Branch delivered letters written by the students of Orchard View Elementary and Virginia Avenue Elementary to the fire fighters, police officers and rescue workers in New York City. The students also sent snacks for the rescue workers and treats for their rescue dogs.

As someone that is familiar with New York City and the surrounding area, it was overwhelming to visit the city after the devastating attacks of September 11, 2001. I felt extreme sorrow, anger and shock as I saw the city in ruins. But I also felt happiness, pride and a sense of belonging when I saw the tremendous outpouring of human kindness. The firefighters, the policemen, the rescue workers, the ordinary people giving up their daily routines to assist in anyway.

New Yorkers are commonly known for their fast paced lives and their rudeness. But as I realized, the entire city has changed, not only externally but internally as well. The roadwork signs on the side of the roads flashed with the phrase "God Bless America," the overpasses on the interstates had American flags hanging from them, the people waved and said hello. The people that I personally encountered were some of the Red Cross workers and policemen. Their gratitude for the letters from all of the children was overwhelming. They were repeatedly thanking me for something I thought was rather small. But as one police officer told me, letters and symbols from different areas of the country are priceless to the workers that have endured this tragedy. I felt a great sense of pride after I left New York, and I can honestly say, first hand, that New York City is not destroyed, it is more alive than it has ever been before.

Jennifer Hall

Jennifer Hall, SFB, pictured with members of the New York City Police Department, New Jersey State Police, and the American Red Cross.

SFB Newsletter (Fall 2001)

Page 98

Appendix H

MEMORANDUM

To: Jimmy Dunne
From: Rod Porter and Georgia Derrico
Re: Sandler O'Neill
Date: August 5, 2004

Jimmy –

You've asked us to reflect on why we chose Sandler O'Neill to represent Southern Financial in our sale to Provident. Georgia's immediate response was that there was never any question that it would be Sandler but that it was important that you understand why. (A lot of this is in our book but I don't think you want to wait for our book signing.)

As you know, Steve Joseph introduced us to Herman Sandler in 1998. For some reason, Herman liked and trusted us. He trusted us in the sense that he invested hundreds of hours of his and the firm's time working with us on things which never earned a penny for Sandler O'Neill. He dissuaded us from becoming an internet bank. He talked us out of doing a fancy preferred stock offering. He spent four hours at dinner one night in Palm Beach trying to talk us out of buying a small leasing company. He didn't succeed that night but after our second day of due diligence we knew he was right.

But it wasn't just Herman, it was deeply ingrained in the culture of the firm. I think we were a profitable client for Steve Joseph on the fixed income side but Steve also did a lot of things for the Bank where Sandler O'Neill never earned a penny. This is in the book but our biggest crisis was a lender liability lawsuit. We were getting contradictory advice from two sets of lawyers. At the peak of the crisis we asked Steve Joseph to come down to Warrenton for the day just to have a cool head with the two of us. It worked.

Ken Puglisi took over the coverage of our stock after 9/11. He was more important than he knows. All of our conference calls were prepared with the foreknowledge that Kenny would ask the toughest questions.

Sandler invited us to the Palm Beach investor conference when the Bank was still tiny. It was extraordinarily useful to listen to the bigger banks and then try to steal their good ideas.

When we realized that the time was coming where we would have to consider selling we knew that you would be personally involved and that was extremely important to us. You always have told us that you either think like an owner or you don't. We knew you think like an owner and we needed that input. You were personally involved throughout the process. You invested time in it long before any of us knew there was going to be a sale.

You will note that we haven't mentioned any of your investment bankers yet. We like a lot of your investment bankers, particularly Tom Duke, but there are a lot of bright investment bankers out there.

The decision wasn't about investment bankers. It was about repaying the trust which Herman and the firm had invested in us and Southern Financial.

Ciao.

Jimmy Dunne Quote-Letter

Page 105

Appendix I

Southern Financial Bank
www.southernfinancialbank.com

Special Edition Newsletter — Fall 1999

Southern Financial & Horizon - Together We're Better!

Southern Financial Bank and The Horizon Bank of Virginia have merged. On October 1st, Southern Financial signage went up at the Horizon branches, the letterhead changed, and business cards were reprinted. But even more importantly, Horizon has joined the Southern Financial family!

As part of our commitment to our new customers and the employees of Horizon Bank, all Horizon employees have been offered positions with the combined institution of Southern Financial. Our new cus-

Southern Financial & Horizon Employees at the Summer Picnic.

tomers will continue to receive the same friendly personal service and also find an array of exciting new products! Southern Financial's customers will also benefit when several new products are offered this fall, including the Southern Financial Debit Card which will be offered to eligible customers in November.

Together, Southern Financial and Horizon can offer customers a wide range of services unmatched by any other bank in Virginia:

Businesses and Consumers
- Convenience—The number of branches where Southern Financial and Horizon customers can bank will increase from 13 branches to 17.
- Online Banking—Southern Financial offers Southern OnLine, Internet banking that makes banking as easy as a click of the mouse! Southern OnLine enables you to check balances, review accounts, confirm deposits, pay bills, and check the status of cleared checks and ATM transactions, and transfer funds – anytime from anywhere!

Consumers
- Discount Brokerage—Southern Financial offers a discount brokerage on the Internet through U.S. Clearing.
- Totally Free Checking—Southern Financial will continue to offer our popular checking account that has no monthly fee, no minimum balance, and unlimited check writing.
- Old Fashioned Savings—Southern Financial also offers our unrivaled savings account with no monthly service charge, no minimum balance, and unlimited withdrawals.
- Visa Card—Southern Financial will adopt Horizon's Visa card program and will offer a new credit card program this fall.
- Online Mortgage Loan Services and Applications—Southern Financial offers convenient mortgage information, including calculators and a reference index.

Businesses
- Larger Lending Limit—Southern Financial's new lending limit is now three times as large as Horizon's was.
- Web Page Design and Hosting—Southern Financial's affiliate, PS Web, provides affordable web design and hosting and the Blue Pages Directory.
- Preferred SBA Lender—Southern Financial is the largest bank SBA lender in Northern Virginia and Horizon Bank established itself as a major business bank in Fairfax County.

SFB Newsletter (Fall 1999)

Page 153

All Proceeds from the sale of this book will be donated to the Michael G Santangelo Jr. Scholarship Fund, a registered 501 (c) 3 organization – Changing Lives One Student at a Time.

For additional information and donations, please visit our website at:

WWW.MICHAELJRFUND.ORG

www.ingramcontent.com/pod-product-compliance
Lightning Source LLC
Chambersburg PA
CBHW040234110526
44582CB00002B/50